In the Shadow of God's Wings

May you always abide in God's love.

Susan Gregg-Schroeder

In the Shadow of God's Wings

*Grace in the Midst of
Depression*

Susan Gregg-Schroeder

UPPER
ROOM BOOKS®
NASHVILLE

Art Direction: Michele Wetherbee
Cover Design: Laura Beers
Cover Photograph: © 1996 William Neill Photography

The Upper Room Web Site: http://www.upperroom.org
Fourth Printing: 2006

Library of Congress Cataloging-in-Publication
Gregg-Schroeder, Susan, 1947–
      In the shadow of God's wings: grace in the midst of depression / Susan Gregg-Schroeder.
          p.   cm.
      Includes bibliographical references.
      ISBN 0-8358-0807-6 (pbk.)
          1. Depressed persons—Religious life. 2. Depression, Mental—Religious aspects—Christianity. 3. Depression, Mental—Case-Patients—Biography.   I. title.
BV4910.34.G74   1997
248.8' 6—dc20   96-43169 CIP

Printed in the United States of America on acid-free paper

This book is dedicated to

my husband, Stan,

my daughter, Sarah,

and my son, Matthew,

for standing by me, for supporting me, and for offering unconditional love during difficult times.

It is also dedicated to

Jim, Jeanne, Mark, Pat, Marc, and Jerry

for their nonjudgmental acceptance
and for walking beside me through the shadow.

Contents

Acknowledgments

WITH SINCERE THANKS and appreciation to Reverend Paul Hetrick, Doris Lumens, and Terri Hamlin for reading my draft, for offering helpful editorial comments, and for sharing the vision of this book with me. A special thank-you to my secretary Judy Phipps whose careful attention to the details of publication made my job easier.

*In the shadow
of your wings
I will take refuge,
until the destroying storms
pass by.*

Psalm 57:1

Prologue

---

*P*EOPLE IN AN AFRICAN VILLAGE purchased a television set. For weeks all of the children, youth, and adults gathered around the television morning, afternoon, and night to watch the programs. Then after a couple of months, the villagers turned the television off and never used it again.

A visitor to the village asked the chief, "Why doesn't anyone watch television?"

"We have decided to listen to the storytellers," the chief replied.

"Doesn't the television know more stories?" the visitor inquired.

"Yes," the chief replied, "but the storyteller knows me."

STORY HAS GREAT POWER, TRANSFORMING POWER. Part of that transforming power comes from the intimacy of storytelling. The stories of our faith heritage, the stories of others, and our own stories make up the fabric of our soul. We learn from stories. We learn what brings joy and pain; what causes anger and sadness; what leads to wholeness of mind, body, and spirit. Stories become windows through which we look at the experiences that have shaped our lives and the lives of others.

Good stories reveal eternal and universal truths. They are a living stream that flows into the deepest recesses of our being. To ignore or discard story is to disconnect ourselves from these universal truths. Only the soul can perceive inner or spiritual realities. Jesus knew this; therefore, he used stories rather than specific explanations, definitions, or terms. Jesus taught through parables; he used symbols and images to represent something not yet known. And so the parables of Jesus contain a wealth of spiritual realities. These stories have retained their relevance and meaning through time, and they continue to speak to a deep place in our souls even today.

Storytelling has lost much of its importance in our contemporary, fast-paced, Internet society. Many children today do not know the nursery rhymes and fairy tales that were such an integral part of my childhood. And I continue to be amazed by the number of children and adults in the church who are unfamiliar with many of the wonderful stories in the Bible.

And yet our society deeply yearns for something most people cannot name. We are spiritual beings, and our spirituality connects us with realities greater than ourselves. People want to feel connected, to sense that they belong. Almost every culture has stories about initiation and rites of passage, rituals that pass on truths from the elders to the young people.

A rich art form has emerged from the Pueblo Indians in New Mexico. Since the 1960s, various artists began creating clay figures of seated "storytellers," surrounded by small children. These pieces of folk art symbolize the passing on of the stories and traditions that connect people of all ages to one another.

One way to find meaning in everyday life is through reading, telling, or listening to story. Stories can be vehicles for change, healing, and unity because most stories are about change. Stories often involve a journey of some kind. And stories, whether oral or written, do not simply involve the storyteller. They involve the listener or the reader in ways known only to him or her. That is the mystery of story.

We may relate the word *story* to the word *re-story* or *restore*, which means to bring the disconnected parts together into a whole. Stories also become "storehouses" for spiritual gifts that await discovery.

An important part of our personal spiritual journey lies in discovering our own story and the spiritual gifts that are "stored away" for us. Families can tell stories of relatives no longer with us on this earth but whose spirits live on through shared story.

Even when we have a wealth of shared family story, we need to develop our own sacred stories. This involves embarking on a journey into our own history that connects us with the "sacred ordinary" of our own daily living. Finding our personal story connects us with an intimate part of ourselves and mysteriously connects us with all humanity and with our God.

Embarking on such a spiritual journey is not without risk. It becomes a journey of faith. As we delve into our own life experiences we may—and I did—discover painful memories. None of us likes pain. In fact we spend a great deal of time avoiding pain. But facing pain, loss, and the chaotic times may move us into new life. And the sharing of that story may provide an entrance into new life for others. Story leads us into life's challenges and carries us through those challenges with a new and different sense of who we are.

And that is what this book is about. For me, writing poetry and story is a form of prayer. It is a means of connecting with my deeper self and with God. I believe that the essence of a spiritual life is shared story. Frederick Buechner, in his book *Telling Secrets*, put it this way:

> Maybe nothing is more important than that we keep track, you and I, of these stories of who we are and where we have come from and the people we have met along the way because it is precisely through these stories in all their particularity, as I have long believed and often said, that God makes [God's] self known to each of us most powerfully and personally. If this is true, it means that to lose track of our stories is to be profoundly impoverished not only humanly but also spiritually.[1]

And so I invite you into my story, a story of my spiritual journey as I dealt with clinical depression. My insights transcend the specifics of my journey and hopefully will touch the lives of all persons who have struggled in the shadow, regardless of the nature of their struggle. Poems are also stories, and throughout the book I share poems I have written during my journey. I invite you now to come along with me as a sojourner in faith.

> Come along with me
>> as a sojourner in faith.
> Bring along
>> a sense of expectancy
>> a vision of high hopes
>> a glimpse of future possibility
>> a vivid imagination
> For God's creation is not done.
>
> We are called to pioneer forth
>> toward a future yet unnamed.
> As we venture forward,
>> we leave behind our desires for
>> a no-risk life
>> worldly accumulations
>> certainty of answers.
>
> Let us travel light
>> in the spirit of faith and expectation
>> toward the God of our hopes and dreams.
>
> Let us be a witness
>> to God's future breaking in.
>
> Come along with me
>> as a sojourner in faith
>> secure in the knowledge
>> that we never travel alone.

1 *Into the* Shadow

FOR ME, SHADOWS AND DARK PLACES have always implied something hidden, mysterious, and forbidden. As a child, I remember playing games of "shadow tag," a game that required bright sunlight. Games of "hide and seek" embraced the hiddenness of the shadow as I sought out dark, secluded places to hide. And I remember the inner clock that told me it was time to go home when the shadows and impending darkness of sunset began to merge into one. In drama, "shadowy" figures usually portray persons to be feared. Shadows serve as an omen of an imminent encounter with the unknown.

As I grew older, the idea of shadow began to take on new meaning as I received comfort from the Psalms. Psalm 17, for example, is a prayer asking God to, "Guard me as the apple of the eye; hide me in the shadow of your wings" (v. 8). We find this image of shadow as protection throughout the Psalms. Psalm 57 begins, "Be merciful to me, O God, be merciful to me, for in you my soul takes refuge; in the shadow of your wings I will take refuge, until the destroying storms pass by." My understanding of shadows has moved from the realm of mystery and forbiddenness to the realm of refuge, of safety, of shelter, and of protection from the unknown and unnamed forces all about me.

However, acceptance of the shadows has not come easily to me, nor has it come quickly. Even as I found comfort in the Psalms, I had no idea that I was about to embark on a journey into the shadows and that "destroying storms" were in my personal weather forecast. As my journey into the shadow began, my immediate impulse was one of resistance. Acceptance came slowly. Only after much pain have I been able to embrace the experience and to see the positive benefits one may gain from the shadows.

Walter Brueggemann has written in *Praying the Psalms* that

> The Psalms mostly do not emerge out of such situations of equilibrium. Rather, people are driven to such poignant prayer and song as are found in the Psalms precisely by *experiences of dislocation and relocation*. It is experiences of being overwhelmed, nearly destroyed, and surprisingly given life which empower us to pray and sing.[1]

In the emotional and psychological realms, the idea of deep darkness and gloom frightens us because it asks us to examine and confront feelings that cause us discomfort or pain. The fact that this examination may lead to profound changes in our lives is also scary.

In psychological terms, shadow is that part of ourselves that we keep hidden in our subconscious. Dr. Carl Jung stated that ninety-five percent of our shadow was pure gold if we would recognize it and name it. Robert Johnson, in his book *Owning Your Own Shadow*, says, "Some of the pure gold of our personality is relegated to the shadow because it can find no place in that great leveling process that is culture."[2] Johnson goes on to say, "To own one's own shadow is to reach a holy place—an inner center—not attainable in any other way. To fail this is to fail one's own sainthood and to miss the purpose of life."[3]

I HAVE BECOME INCREASINGLY INTERESTED in Celtic spirituality, which has many of the same foundational beliefs as Native American spirituality. It reflects a groundedness in nature, in the changing of seasons, and in the interrelatedness of all creation. David Adam has written a book of modern prayers in the Celtic tradition entitled *Tides and Seasons*. He speaks of the winter's being a time of barrenness and death. Yet winter is also a time of beauty and a time of purifying because only then do we see things we may never have seen before.

In the British Isles the winters are harsh, the trees are bare; animals and people need extra protection to survive. The Celts would surround themselves with loved ones. They would use the index finger of their right hand and, pointing the finger to all the people gathered, they would turn around in a full circle sunward. It reminded them that even in the darkness, God always surrounds us. David Adam writes this poem entitled "Come, Creator":

> *From chaos and emptiness,*
> *From loneliness and lifelessness,*
> > *Come, Creator, Come.*
>
> *From darkness and shapelessness.*
> *From the abyss and awfulness,*
> > *Come, Creator, Come.*
>
> *From fearfulness and hopelessness,*
> *From weakness and dreadfulness,*
> > *Come, Creator, Come.*[4]

AT TIMES EACH OF US ENTERS THE WINTER, the darkness, the shadows of life. Mine came when I was into my third year of ministry at a large urban church. My ministry was going well. I was excited about my new career and the many opportunities for serving others that had opened up to me. I enjoyed being part of a large staff and felt confident of my abilities as the only female clergy member. My colleagues were supportive and encouraging, and I had no doubt that I had made the right decision when I left classroom teaching to become an ordained minister.

GROWING SADNESS

Then my life slowly began to change. I experienced a deep sadness, but I wasn't sure why. The news that my birth father was quite ill triggered part of the sadness. My parents had divorced when I was very young. Although my birth father hadn't been a tangible part of my life, I realized that his illness might cut short our opportunity to establish a relationship. My birth mother had died of breast cancer after a lingering illness when I was sixteen. I suddenly had anxiety that I was going to be all alone— that I was going to be an orphan. The word *orphan* became a trigger for a deep inner pain and fear.

At the same time, our country's increasing involvement in the Middle East situation eventually led to the Gulf War in early 1991. I watched CNN obsessively. I couldn't believe we were actually going to war. Many of our parishioners were leaving for the battlefields. I remember blessing the rings of a couple I had married as they awaited their military orders.

Gnawing Fear

I felt a gnawing fear as well as a growing sadness. I'd grown up in the fifties and sixties, and I vividly recalled the fear of war, especially the fear of nuclear war. Memories of air raid drills— of having to crawl under the school desks with hands over our heads and faces—came to mind. I knew persons who had built nuclear fallout shelters in their backyards. I remember their discussions about who would be allowed to enter those shelters and who would be turned away. My own response to these fearful possibilities was to create a secret hiding place in the dark recesses of my closet where I kept food, blankets, water, and other necessities to "protect" my family. I would sneak cans of food from the kitchen and fill empty bottles with water.

The Gulf War threatened my sense of security and safety. I became more protective of my own children and more concerned about everyday security and safety issues. I installed dead-bolt locks and solid-core doors. But, as I soon learned, the roots of my fear went much deeper.

Most of us are familiar with the phrase from Psalm 23: "the valley of the shadow of death" (KJV). The New Revised Standard

Version of the Bible translates the phrase as "darkest valley." A
more accurate translation comes from the Akkadian word *sala-
mu*, which means "to grow black." We might accurately trans-
late "shadow of death" as "gloom" or "deep darkness." And one
definition of shadow is "very close to or verging upon." I was
very close to something I could not name. None of my pastoral
counseling classes in seminary prepared me for the deep darkness into which I was about to enter.

DIMINISHING SELF-CONFIDENCE

Another subtle change came in my self-confidence. While I had
been relatively comfortable leading worship in our large congregation, I began to feel tense, awkward, and insecure. My initial reaction to these new feelings was to analyze what was happening and why I was reacting this way. Rather than listening to
and trusting the stirrings in my heart, I became afraid. I feared
being abandoned, being orphaned, and being alone. Since the
opposite of fear is trust, I turned to my faith for help. But my
strong need to control, analyze, and understand caused me to
question even my trust in a loving God. Whom could I trust?
Faith stances that I had formerly taken for granted were suddenly shaky.

Several friends suggested that I find a spiritual director who
would guide me through the changes in my personal and spiritual life. A spiritual director or guide is a person trained to help
an individual prayerfully discern the subtle movements of the
Holy Spirit in his or her life and to offer encouragement and
support in times of change and transition. All of this occurs
within the context of prayer. Christian traditions in the fourth
and fifth centuries, especially in the monastic communities,
practiced spiritual direction.

With the advent of modern psychology, psychiatrists and
therapists all but replaced spiritual direction. Faith in God
became secondary to faith in those trained in science. Pastoral
counselors emerged as a unique blending of the two disciplines.

But some important differences remain between pastoral counseling and spiritual direction. People turn to pastoral counselors more often in times of crisis or emotional stress, while spiritual direction is a continuous process that involves the healthy as well as the hurting. The pastoral counseling model frequently takes place in an office-based setting rather than in the church or community. Spiritual direction grounds itself more in the liturgical and sacramental framework of the Body of Christ.

Only recently has the art of spiritual direction received more attention as persons yearn for a closer relationship with God. Because I discerned the importance of bringing a prayerful dimension to my counseling, I chose someone trained in both disciplines.

I chose a spiritual director who also happened to be a minister and a licensed counselor. We began meeting every other week, and our explorations centered around issues of trust. Our goal was to look at the stirrings of the spirit within and to seek discernment regarding the changes I was feeling called to make. We worked on letting go, on releasing, on setting healthy boundaries. I began to examine my childhood intensely for the first time, and it was painful.

Examining the Past

I began to understand that my mother's love for me had been conditional, based on my behavior and performance. As a result, pleasing people had become an addiction. Because of my parents' early divorce and my mother's lingering illness and eventual death when I was sixteen, abandonment issues were real. I had perfectionist tendencies; control was important. I felt I had to measure up somehow to others' expectations. I discovered that while I had developed many skills to care for others, I was helpless to care for myself. My old ways of coping weren't working anymore.

I also began to understand that I carried many destructive messages from my mother with me; messages that blocked my becoming the person God intended. My wise spiritual director encouraged me to complete a simple exercise that became an important symbol in my journey. He advised me to write down all the negative messages I had received from my mother. I was to give "the list" to him as I walked down the aisle the following Sunday to lead worship, knowing that someone else could hold those destructive messages for that hour.

As I sat down to write that list, the ugly words flowed onto the page effortlessly. They were so familiar; they had been a part of who I was for so long. I cried after reading the list, realizing that I was still trying to gain my mother's approval and love. I passed the list to my spiritual director the following Sunday, and we made a covenant that he would hold the list for me until I was ready to let it go.

THE GULF WAR ENDED, BUT THE WAR WITHIN ME continued. I met with my spiritual director for the next six months. I risked sharing some of my struggle with my senior pastor and a few close friends. Their support and concern helped me limp along. What amazed me was that the church in general had no idea what I was going through. In fact, many people noted that the "performance" of my church duties was exceptionally good.

But all was soon to change. A sudden series of losses was about to plunge me into the depths of darkness I had read about in the Psalms. I sought comfort in a retreat center and discovered a series of tapes on child abuse. Even though I knew somewhere deep inside that my mother had abused me emotionally and physically, I had stuffed that information away in an inaccessible place. I had focused my attention on my marriage and the building of our family with our children.

When I listened to the tapes on child abuse, the painful memories flooded in and overwhelmed me. Like many other abuse victims, I had denied the abuse. I had elevated my mother to a standard no person could ever attain.

Many studies indicate that persons abused as children often

continue the cycle and become abusers as adults. I am thankful that my first career as a kindergarten teacher enabled me to break that cycle of violence. During my years of teaching, I learned alternative ways of dealing with disciplinary issues in my classroom. The many classes offered in child development and classroom management taught me how to deal with anger in a constructive way.

GOD'S UNCONDITIONAL LOVE

When my first child was born, my husband gave me a beautiful clay sculpture of a mother and child. That was the first piece of what became an extensive collection of mother and child sculptures, paintings, and other works of art. This collection symbolized for me God's unconditional love. It became one vehicle by which I protected myself from the truth; I created an idealized mother image. I displayed this collection and talked about its meaning at many church groups. I was even able to write a poem about Mother's Day.

> It's Mother's Day again . . . a time to acknowledge
>   those qualities that hopefully we try
>   to live up to every day of the year.
>
> An ideal Mother is available to . . .
>   provide for physical needs
>   care for the sick
>   teach right from wrong
>   be on call 24 hours a day
>   keep her children safe and secure
>   answer hundreds of questions
>   encourage each new growth
>   listen to every need
>   love unconditionally.
> God must be a Mother!

After listening to the tapes on child abuse, I began to realize the deep-seated lie I had perpetuated, and the truth hit hard. My mother had done none of the things I had written about. The truth was that I did not feel safe and secure as a child. My mother took out her anger at my birth father on me. Most important, I realized my mother's love was conditional. I wanted to smash and destroy my beautiful mother-and-child collection. I even began to doubt God's unconditional love for me.

During this tumultuous time I received word that my birth father had died the day before. My stepfather had adopted me at an early age, but I had recently been working to establish a relationship with my birth father, my two half-sisters, and other members of my paternal birth family. With my startling realization of my mother's abuse and the phone call relating my birth-father's death, I felt as if both of my parents had died the same day. I was totally numb.

My husband and I traveled to participate in my father's service and visited neighbors and the house where I had been born in Oakland. We took numerous pictures of my old neighborhood, my birth house, and the lake near the nursery school I attended. At my birth father's service, I met my half-sister and learned that she had breast cancer.

A week later I awoke to the newspaper headlines' telling of perhaps the worst firestorm in recent U.S. history. A devastating fire roared through the Oakland/Berkeley hills, fueled by high winds and hot, dry air. The human toll of dead and injured was enormous, coupled with the loss of more than 3,350 houses and apartments. It took me two days to confirm that my birth house and the house of our neighbors had been totally destroyed. That day was my birthday. I realized that I was now the same age my mother had been when she died. Even more disturbing was the fact that my daughter was sixteen—my age when my mother died.

SYMPTOMS OF DEPRESSION

The symptoms were there, but I didn't recognize what was happening to me. Sadness and despair overwhelmed me. I felt disoriented and disconnected from my feelings and myself. I did not want to eat; I couldn't sleep. Nothing I did brought any pleasure; I was simply going through the motions. All I wanted to do was isolate myself from everyone. Any task I attempted took great effort. I felt utterly hopeless about the future. Soon I got to the point of believing that life was not worth living, and I developed an elaborate suicide plan. Yet, at the same time, I couldn't concentrate or think clearly. I felt as if I were falling into a bottomless black hole, and I saw no way out. I avoided the people who could help me most.

Fortunately, some people around me recognized the symptoms of severe clinical depression. I had several offers of help, but I felt such shame that I couldn't respond. After all, I was a professional, the one who was supposed to be helping others. I finally agreed to talk to a psychiatrist who belonged to the church. It was one of the most humbling experiences of my life. As the only female minister in a large church, I had put forth a great deal of effort to "prove" that I was capable of handling my ministerial responsibilities—only to find myself weeping uncontrollably in a parishioner's medical office. He suggested medication and recommended hospitalization. I reluctantly agreed to try medication but clearly stated my position, "I would rather be dead than have to go to the hospital."

The next week was a blur as I tried to keep up the pretense of working. I visited my regular doctor to get medication, and he immediately referred me to the psychosocial services offered by my health plan. Hospitalization was again recommended. My husband and I were so run down from trying to make it through each day that I reluctantly agreed.

HOSPITALIZATION

The first night in the hospital I never slept. I paced the floors, wondering what I was doing there. After all, I had visited parishioners in this place. Everything was backwards. As a person of faith, I felt I should be able to work myself out of this mess. I still sought control. I didn't tell anyone on the unit that I was a minister, and I lived in constant fear of being recognized. It was like leading a double life.

Fortunately, I was in one of the finest psychiatric hospitals available. Within a few days I was transferred to the Cognitive Therapy unit. I took a detached position and became an observer. I found myself analyzing the presentations of the various professionals, and I related them to my own counseling work at the church. Perhaps I could learn something that would help in my ministry.

This approach to therapy was my way of denying and avoiding my own problems. I rarely participated in therapy groups, focusing instead on becoming the model patient. After two weeks on the unit, I was discharged.

My discharge came just before the Thanksgiving holiday. I was still numb, disconnected, and very depressed. I was required to go to aftercare meetings at the hospital. In these meetings it became clear that my suicidal ideations continued. One week after discharge, I was readmitted.

My first day back in the psychiatric hospital, I was walking the exercise track with the other patients. I suddenly realized that the hospital where I had done my clinical pastoral education (CPE) was just next door. I felt a real need to connect with my CPE supervisor and to visit the chapel that was so familiar to me. I sensed an urgent need for a spiritual connection in this time of great turmoil. So I set out for the chapel in the adjacent hospital, thinking no one would miss me for such a short time.

I returned to the track before our group time was up and began participating in the next activity—art therapy. I quietly painted sun catchers; and while feeling deeply introspective, I tried to sort out all that had precipitated my unexpected hospital readmittance.

The phone rang, and a nurse called me from the room. I was "greeted" by a male nurse whom I knew and respected. He told me that the hospital had received notification of my leaving the grounds and had called my doctor. Because I seemed to lack "impulse control," I was being taken to the Intensive Care Unit—a locked unit. Four large male attendants literally dragged me to a room in the locked ICU. I was told to take my clothes off for a strip search. If I did not agree to the search, attendants would forcibly restrain me in order to carry it out. Sobbing uncontrollably and refusing to be touched, I felt I had no options. I submitted to the most humiliating experience of my life.

After that initial ordeal, I was left alone on the ward. I found a small consulting room; I remember crawling into the corner and remaining there in a fetal position. My stomach hurt, and vivid childhood memories of myself crouching in the corner of the kitchen flooded my mind. I could feel again my mother kicking me in the stomach and my helplessness in stopping the attack. The louder I cried in protest, the angrier my mother became. I had learned as a child to "shut down" and choke the sobs somewhere deep inside.

Another patient from the unit approached me. She began stroking my hair and making comments of a sexual nature. Dazed and confused, I found myself utterly helpless to protest her advances, and no staff person came to protect me. A patient I had come to know on the open unit came to my rescue.

I knew that I had to get out of that place or I would go crazy. I felt intense rage, frustration, and total helplessness. My social worker became my advocate, calling both my husband and my doctor. It took several hours, but my doctor finally agreed to release me from the ICU.

I returned to another open unit. The next day a psychiatrist "evaluated" me. To this day, I am not sure if anyone really understood that I had left the track because of my need for spiritual connection. I still have nightmares about that experience, but it was the beginning of an awareness that treatment for my depression needed to be more than just clinical care. My spiritual needs had to be addressed as well, but it would be months before I would be able to articulate those needs.

I was so far down at that point that I let myself be a patient. Learning that there were other professional people in the unit, I finally shared with a few of them that I was a minister. However, I had to guard against taking on that role with the other patients in my unit who sought me out for spiritual guidance. I had to admit that I needed help as much as they did; I was working hard at chipping away some of the anger and grief that was causing my numbness. One doctor suggested that I write letters to my deceased mother; I practiced assertiveness techniques. And, at the suggestion of my psychiatrist, I found someone with whom I could do psychotherapy. I began feeling more at peace and was discharged a few days before Christmas.

While in the hospital, I could not let go of my work responsibilities. I would get a weekend pass to spend Saturday at the office. I continued to participate in Sunday services because the congregation did not know of my hospitalization.

After the first of the year I attended a day treatment program several times a week, still managing to keep up with my work and to have a smiling face on Sundays. I remember coming across an editorial in a newspaper on depression entitled, "You seem so normal." The effort and pain it took to keep the appearance of normalcy was overwhelming, and I would usually spend Sunday afternoon in bed—recovering from the extra pressure of "being normal" Sunday mornings.

THERAPY

After my discharge from the hospital, I entered therapy, which turned out to be a painfully slow process. Because of my deep spiritual needs, I chose a therapist who is also a pastoral counselor and an ordained minister. For about six months I was in therapy once a week, and I continued meeting with my spiritual director twice a month.

My spiritual director's move out of state triggered another difficult period. Even though I intellectually understood his moving, it surfaced those tender feelings of abandonment. And he took with him the symbolic "list." Building trust with my new pastoral counselor/therapist was a long, slow process. Almost two years would pass before I could ask my spiritual director to send the list back to me so I could give it to my current pastoral counselor.

I WISH I COULD SAY THAT MY DEPRESSION magically left, but I can't. It has been a continuing struggle with bouts of depression as I have worked in therapy through some difficult childhood issues. I was not one of those who found the right medication on the first try, and thyroid problems further complicated my chemical imbalance. I was admitted to the hospital twice more over the next two years.

Over time I have come to understand my depression as a chronic condition. Statistics clearly indicate that persons who have subsequent episodes of depression are more likely to have episodes in the future. Like other chronic illnesses, such as diabetes or high blood pressure, depression requires consistent monitoring. I have accepted the fact that I will probably be taking medication for my depression for a long time—if not the rest of my life. But I've also learned the warning signs of a downward spiral and have gained some coping skills.

The second two admissions to the hospital were by my choice. While I did have that one dreadful ICU experience, overall, I found the hospital to be a haven of safety and a respite from the pressures of the outside world. I felt secure, nurtured, and free of expectations and responsibilities. I didn't have to worry about planning meals or doing the laundry or picking up kids from school. I had to let go of control and focus on myself for a change. And I was grateful for a supportive staff that was willing to talk any time I needed to. I also learned a great deal from the other patients, so that I didn't feel so isolated in my depression.

I experienced many moments of deep pain—psychologically, physically, and spiritually. Psychologically, I felt that I had died and that the deep despair I felt would never end. I had physical symptoms of anxiety, panic, and pain. I often felt physical pain in my stomach, as well as nausea. I felt abandoned by God. I felt totally helpless, overwhelmed, and alone. In the darkness of the shadow, I wrote my own psalm of lament, "Psalm 151":

O God, I feel like an orphan.
Even the word orphan
is too painful to speak.
The word brings up past memories
I'd rather keep hidden in dark places.

I feel abandoned by my earthly parents
through death and circumstances
beyond my control.
I fear the emptiness inside me
the darkness around me.
I even fear the light trying to break in.
I am the frightened child
trembling in the corner
alone and forgotten.

I yearn for safety
for security
for sureness of the presence
of one who loves me as I am
who loves me without conditions
without expectations.

My faith tells me that you, O God,
are my loving parent,
and I am your beloved child. I know that in my head.
But when I grope around the dark corners
of my heart,

I find only emptiness
>   *estrangement*
>   *exile.*

My futile attempts to seek your presence
>   *leave me even more alone*
>>   *more deserted*
>>   *more separated*
>   *from your healing love.*

I cry out to you, O God.
Adopt this orphaned child as your own.

I had descended into hell. The Apostles' Creed suddenly took on new meaning and significance for me—Jesus descended into hell. And I was in my own personal hell. I could not will my way out of this deep darkness, and so I had to learn how to abide in the shadow.

2 Abiding in the Shadow

*T*HE "VALLEY OF THE SHADOW OF DEATH" is difficult to describe to those who have not spent time wandering in that deep darkness. Many people have tried. Sir Winston Churchill who suffered with depression throughout his life called it a "black dog." Writer William Styron has written of the depression that almost ended his life in his book *Darkness Visible*. Among the images he uses to describe his depression are "drowning suffocation," "helpless stupor," "unfocused dread," "storm of the mind," and "despair beyond despair." In reference to Dante's *Inferno*, Styron says, "For those who have dwelt in depression's dark wood, and known its inexplicable agony, their return from the abyss is not unlike the ascent of the poet, trudging upward and upward out of hell's black depths and at last emerging into what he saw as 'the shining world.'"[1]

My descent into hell was straight down. I struggle with unipolar depression rather than manic or bipolar depression. With unipolar depression, a person feels depressed all the time instead of experiencing the false highs and sudden plunges often associated with bipolar depression. I was frequently overwhelmed—as if giant waves were breaking over me—without hope of finding a way out of the dark depths. I also felt disconnected from myself. I no longer knew who Susan was. It seemed that my soul became an internal battleground populated by unseen foes.

31

NAMING THE PAIN

There comes a point when one must name the pain if one chooses to begin the journey into the light. Naming those unseen foes to myself was a beginning. I began to name my demons, my dragons, my monsters. They lurk as betrayal, abandonment, rejection, worthlessness, fear of trusting anyone—even God. When I first began to name the pain to myself, I wrote the following poem entitled "Monsters."

> *They crept up ever so quietly*
> > *leaving only hints of their presence*
> > *cautious to avoid the light.*
>
> *I wanted to flee*
> > *to run toward the light*
> > *even to destroy these lurking enemies within.*
>
> *But something caused me to wait.*
>
> *Perhaps the monsters know something I don't know.*
> *Perhaps they could be guides to explore*
> > *those secret, hidden places deep inside.*
>
> *Perhaps I could learn from them.*
> *Perhaps we could get to know one another*
> > *. . . just a little.*
>
> *Perhaps they even have names.*
>
> *If I'm going to be with these monsters, O God,*
> > *I need the assurance of Your presence.*
>
> *You know my fears.*
> *Nothing is hidden from You.*
> *If I decide to meet these monsters, O God,*
> > *please stand beside me*
> > *. . . and hold my hand.*

PROCESSING THE GRIEF

The journey through depression, or "dark night of the soul," is similar in many ways to the stages of grief described by Elisabeth Kübler-Ross. All of us experience this grief process at different times in our lives whether through the death of a loved one, the breakup of a relationship, or the loss of a job. We may experience grief in times of major transition—a move to another city, children's leaving home, gradual loss of health in the aging process, or the need to come to terms with our personal limitations.

In the grief process we go through the stages of denial and isolation, anger, bargaining, depression, and finally acceptance at our own pace and in our own way. Depression thrusts us into the grief process because a significant part of ourselves is in the throes of death. The passage through these stages does not follow a neat progression. Life is never that simple!

DENIAL AND ISOLATION

First of all, for me, there was major denial. The doctors had it all wrong. They did not understand. I did not need medication, and I certainly did not need to be hospitalized. I just needed some time and space. I could work things out myself if people would just give me a chance.

Denial surfaces because facing the truth about ourselves is a difficult and daunting task. It is easier to live with our fantasies. The suicide of prominent persons often surprise us because, through denial, they have been able to function in their jobs and hide their inner pain.

Isolation often accompanies denial. I experienced most comfort when in bed with the covers over my head. Healthful time alone and the isolation of depression differ greatly. My isolation was not healthy, and it became a way of hiding from or avoiding the reality of my depression.

ANGER

Anger is another stage through which I passed and continue to pass in my healing process. Anger is an ongoing struggle for many of us. When I hear insensitive comments about depression, I get angry. I was, and still am, bombarded with comments such as "You've got so much going for you," "Look at the positive side of things," "Just snap out of it." And my favorite: "You should exercise."

While physical exercise often benefits persons suffering from depression, placing "shoulds" on a depressed person simply makes the person feel guilty, more depressed, and eventually more angry. I still find myself reacting too quickly, or even inappropriately, to people's insensitive comments. I began to identify triggers that touched internal, vulnerable places that I could not yet name.

Yet anger does not come easily to me. I struggled while writing a sermon on the text of Jesus' overturning the tables of the money changers in the Temple. Because this story appears in all four Gospels, it is hard to ignore. Preparing my sermon, I realized that Jesus too had buttons that could be pushed. Seeing the busy, bustling scene in the Temple courtyard, Jesus suddenly was struck by the futility of all that activity. He was struck by the waste, the deception, and the manipulation for selfish human purposes. Maybe he saw the sickness in the religious institution and felt that he could not remain silent. He got mad and expressed that anger in very physical acts. This raw anger makes many of us squirm a bit.

Despite my preaching on this text, I struggled to express my "holy anger." I would get angry at someone, either from my childhood or present situations, and would be overcome with guilt for being angry. I would then get angry at myself and become convinced that the person with whom I was angry would reject or abandon me.

As a rule, the church has not been particularly helpful in

teaching us how to express anger appropriately. Many of us feel guilty about our anger. We hear so many sermons on love, reconciliation, and forgiveness that we suppress our anger. I accepted the classical church teaching that equated anger with sin. After all, we've been taught that anger is one of the seven "deadly" sins. From the Sermon on the Mount in Matthew 5, we recall the words, "If you are angry with a brother or sister, you will be liable to judgment" (v. 22). The writer of Ephesians states, "Do not let the sun go down on your anger" (4:26) or "put away from you . . . all anger, . . forgiving one another, as God in Christ has forgiven you" (4:31-32).

But we also cannot ignore scripture that confronts us with a God whose anger not only pervades the Hebrew Scriptures but enters the New Testament as well. The story of the money-changers is a text where Jesus clearly expresses anger. To sidestep the issue of anger because it makes us feel uncomfortable is to ignore the fullness of the Word of God.

I must admit that I don't always embrace anger courageously. Often I push down my anger. Instead of directing my anger into constructive channels, I direct my anger toward myself. This misdirection results in increased feelings of worthlessness, in guilt, and even in suicidal ideations.

Like many people, I've learned to avoid confrontation by excusing others' behavior or by accepting the guilt or blame myself. Many of us have been taught to deny or repress anger; we want to please others. Women particularly evidence this desire to please. Harriet Lerner has written a *New York Times* best-selling book about women and anger entitled *The Dance of Anger*. She writes,

> Most of us have received little help in learning to use our anger to clarify and strengthen ourselves and our relationships. Instead, our lessons have encouraged us to fear anger excessively, to deny it entirely, to displace it onto inappropriate targets, or to turn it against ourselves.[2]

Through many societal and church teachings, I've internalized the belief that anger is unacceptable. It is the opposite of forgiveness and is, therefore, a nonspiritual reaction. But I am learning that anger is an important aspect of our spiritual journey and that healthy anger can be holy anger. It is not what we feel that is sinful; it is what we do with our feelings. Holy, righteous anger can serve as a powerful catalyst for change. We in the church can transform anger into energy for love by providing available avenues for the expression of anger in healthy ways.

Flora Slosson Wuellner is a retreat leader, spiritual guide, and ordained minister in the United Church of Christ. Her book *Heart of Healing, Heart of Light* has helped me learn to deal with my anger. Reverend Wuellner talks about two major forms of anger. The first she calls "infected anger." Infected anger is murky and unclear; we aren't really sure at whom or at what we are angry. We just know that we are angry. Often something quite minor can trigger infected anger, and we explode or lash out in a destructive way. Infected anger may be individual or communal, and persons may easily manipulate this anger to target certain individuals or groups.

Reverend Wuellner calls the other kind of anger "clear" anger. She describes it as "the clean, healthy flame of outraged justice and humanity."[3] This anger has a cause, a reason that we know and acknowledge. She states,

> This anger can be a powerful, creative energy for defiance of evil, for decision making, for protection of self and others, and for limit-setting. It is out of this clear anger that forgiveness and reconciliation from healthy roots can eventually rise.[4]

I am coming to understand that facing anger and being open to its transforming and healing power is part of my spiritual journey. Clear anger calls us to confront and stop abuse and injustice of all kinds, as Jesus did.

Clear anger, or what I call holy anger, can communicate with and even convert others toward a vision of God's kingdom. Holy anger can unite us in a common purpose. I'm reminded of a verse from a poem by Dylan Thomas:

> *Do not go gentle into that good night.*
> *Rage, rage against the dying of the light.*[5]

Our baptism calls us to rage against the night; to battle the forces of evil, injustice, and oppression in whatever forms they present themselves. Slowly I am learning to embrace anger as a God-given emotion, both individually and collectively. Anger is an emotional energy deep within us that signals a warning that all is not right. Anger demands a change of some sort. Thus, anger has the power to move us enough so that we disrupt the status quo and challenge the injustice or wrong that touches us so deeply. It takes tremendous courage to embrace such a powerful emotion, but the courage comes when we truly believe that anger is God's gift.

BARGAINING

Along with denial and anger, another stage of grief is the bargaining stage. I believed that if I did everything right, I would get better—if I prayed the right way, if I followed my doctor's orders, if I said the "right" things in therapy, and if I participated appropriately in the hospital program, my depression would magically disappear.

I was stuck on the control issue: I would be saved by my own "works." My bargaining with God in prayer was simply another way of trying to control God. But in the end, bargaining only leads to a feeling of total helplessness. My futile attempts to "fix" things caused greater grief; and, in the darkest times, forced my dependence on God's grace moving in the shadow. Abiding in the shadow is abiding in helplessness. The most difficult lesson I am still learning is that "being" and not "doing" is what allows me to be open enough to accept God's presence working to bring about real healing.

Depression

The fourth stage of grief, depression, was a constant companion. I experienced little relief. I felt helpless to meet my family's needs when I could not even take care of myself.

I think my husband, Stan, and I both had hoped my depression would just go away, especially after the first round of medication. It soon became obvious that we could no longer deal with my illness alone. Stan missed work so that I would not be left alone. He handled all my medications and emptied the medicine cabinet of anything that could be potentially harmful. The decision to enter the hospital the first time came partly because Stan was worn down from taking care of me.

After Stan and I decided that I would enter the hospital, we went out to dinner as a family to tell our children. Our daughter knew more of what was going on, but we had not been open about my depression with our son. I'll never forget my son's reaction as we sat in the restaurant: Matthew let out a big sigh of relief. "I'm so glad," he said. "I thought you were going to tell me that you had cancer." From that moment on, Stan and I were totally honest with our children about what was going on. They visited the hospital with us prior to my admission. They needed the assurance that it was not at all like *One Flew over the Cuckoo's Nest*.

Our family life experienced many changes. Stan was my constant traveling companion through the shadow as both of us learned to adapt to this illness. Each change brought difficulty. First came our admission that I had a serious, life-threatening problem. We had decisions to make, and each decision led to others. We dealt with doctor's appointments, medications, and hospitalizations. After being advised to find a therapist, we undertook the many steps involved in that process.

New Role Definition

Stan, like many of us, started out with a solution-oriented approach: If we just get the right combination of medication and therapy, things will be all right. He read extensively about depression and approached it in a logical manner.

Our marriage roles changed dramatically when we realized there was no quick solution to my depression. Stan was forced to take on a parental role to protect me from myself. He was always assessing the situation, watching for clues, and making difficult decisions. At times during my periods of severe instability, he took action and denied me access to my car. He stood firm through all my protestations when he felt I was in danger.

Stan also put away all medications. Because of my need for control, periodically he would put some medications back to allow me a sense that things were getting better. In these depths of depression, I wanted desperately to stop the pain of my unrelenting despair, even if it ultimately would lead to my death. In those dark moments, I could not even fathom the effect suicide would have had on my family. I only knew that I had to stop the pain.

During this time my husband's work situation became more demanding and stressful; yet he was hesitant to burden me with his problems. He met with a counselor for about eight months and began to recognize his own anger and disappointment that other people did not understand the urgency of our situation. Our pain was neither recognized nor understood by those from virtually every arena—family, friends, coworkers, and the church. Our initial attempts to hide my depression were partially responsible. But the response was minimal, even from those in whom we confided. This was true even after I wrote an open letter to the church about my depression. The stigma of depression and other mental illnesses remains strong, and people seldom know how to react.

Recently I broke a small bone in my foot and had to walk around with a cast and cane. Interestingly, I received more sympathetic concern over this tiny broken bone than I ever had with my broken spirit and wounded soul. Rosalynn Carter has written an excellent article, "A Voice for the Voiceless—the Church and the Mentally Ill." She points out that people expect the minister, priest, or rabbi to have it all together. She contends that this expectation is a major contributing factor to clergy burnout.

When clergy or other helping professionals reveal their problems, the church does not know how to respond. She writes, "Those in a position to make a decision about these caregivers sometimes respond by pretending that a crisis doesn't exist. Other times they believe that the caregiver's move to another locale will resolve all the problems. Too often churches have sought to ignore a simple reality: that mental illness can come even to those who are providing care."[6]

Persons in positions of leadership, prominence, or caregiving are not immune to depression. Often others do not realize the degree of their personal pain because they continue to function in their respective places of work. I've been encouraged that well-known persons like Mike Wallace, Rod Steiger, Joan Rivers, Dick Cavett, and Kathy Cronkite, to name a few, have courageously told their stories. But, at the same time, I am painfully aware of the silence of many of my clergy colleagues and others in the helping professions who do not reveal their personal struggles for fear of losing their jobs.

But depression among leaders and caring persons is nothing new. I am reminded of the story of the prophet Elijah as told in 1 Kings 18 and 19. Worship of the pagan idol Baal had become widespread in Israel, and Elijah tried to restore the worship of Yahweh. After a dramatic showdown with the priests of Baal on Mount Carmel in which Elijah was victorious, Queen Jezebel, sympathetic to Baal worship, threatened his life.

Elijah left his servant and fled to the desert where he took refuge under a broom tree. He wished he would die. Instead of gathering friends around him for support, he isolated himself. Elijah, the prophet, was experiencing many of the symptoms of depression: lack of sleep, physical exhaustion, isolation, and irrational negative thinking about his own death.

Elijah's story reveals some helpful ways that God brought Elijah out of his depression—steps that are equally helpful today. God didn't criticize Elijah or tell him his depression was a sin. God didn't tell Elijah to just "snap out of it" and get back to his work. Instead, an angel came and ministered to him: Elijah was given food and drink, and then he was allowed to sleep.

The nonjudgmental way the angel came and gave him food especially touches me. I dislike cooking and cook only out of necessity. At the depths of my own depression, I, like Elijah, pulled back and isolated myself. I could not eat, and I too got caught up in my own negative thought patterns. And, like Elijah, I often wished I was dead. I was unable to fix dinner for my family, much less do the laundry and other household tasks. How I wished an "angel" had left some food by my broom tree!

Faith Community as Minister

Elijah's story reveals important insights as to how the community of faith can minister to persons suffering from depression. Compassion and understanding instead of criticism and unrealistic expectations will help depressed persons know they are not alone, even when they feel alone. The offering of food and drink not only nourishes the physical body, but, like the Eucharist, provides a ritual dimension of spiritual nourishment. Later in Elijah's story—when he is ready—he is encouraged to talk about his experience and his worries. Nonjudgmental listening is a gift the church community can give depressed persons. Cards or notes simply saying the person is being held in prayer are much appreciated.

Many days later God questions Elijah about his purposes and encourages Elijah to come out of the cave on Mount Horeb to which he had retreated. As Elijah stands on the mountain the wind gusts mightily, an earthquake shakes the mountain, and fire rages. God was not in the wind, the earthquake, or the fire;

Elijah discovered the Lord in the "sound of sheer silence." God restored in Elijah a realistic hope—hope that with God's help he could accomplish the tasks set before him.

Unfortunately, Stan and I were not ministered to by angels, and we had to learn how to deal with my depression by trial and error. We learned that recovery from depression is not linear, and it follows no predictable path. Stan, who spent his early childhood years in Michigan, likened our journey to "skating on thin ice." When individuals first learn to skate, experienced skaters (those who know where the ice is strong enough to hold their body weight) guide them. And so, like nonskaters, we slipped, fell, and occasionally broke through the ice to the cold, murky depths below.

For a person like Stan who is more comfortable with logical solutions to problems, our journey was uncertain and frightening. Stan had to move into the role of being caregiver to a person to whom others looked for support. The hardest part for me was to let go of my need for control and to allow my husband to take care of me when I was unable to care for myself. But we have walked through the valley of the shadow of death together and have grown much closer through that experience. Stan's love for me has been a constant, especially when I could not love myself. And that love has contributed greatly to my healing.

Stan learned a lot from our experience with depression. For me, the most helpful change was his transition from offering solutions to being a presence. When no one else had any idea what we were going through, cards from my husband would show up in the most unlikely places, assuring me of his love and offering hope. His daily calls to "check in" and his love offerings of flowers brightened my day.

Reaching Out for Help
Many depression sufferers do not have a supportive caregiver standing with them through the dark times. I worked with the

singles' ministry at my church for many years and witnessed the difficulty of those without support systems. We worked hard to make our singles' group a safe place where persons could share their pain and receive support from others who had gone through similar experiences. It is important that depressed persons reach out and find a support person or group so that they know they are not alone or unique in facing their darkness.

This is asking a lot of a person in severe depression. Many of us resist asking for help, but reaching out for help is especially difficult for someone experiencing the feelings of shame, worthlessness, and isolation that often accompany depression. Yet it must be done. If the first attempt fails, keep on trying. Help is out there. As the body of Christ, we are meant to be in community and to be a presence to those who are hurting. Paul states in Galatians 6:2, "Bear one another's burdens, and in this way you will fulfill the law of Christ." Learning to reach out and allow others to care for us is just as important as our willingness to care for others.

Discerning the Changing Season

Ecclesiastes 3 begins with the familiar words, "For everything there is a season, and a time for every matter under heaven." Discerning the season's changing became a challenge. Eventually a counselor advised Stan that his constant attentiveness, while necessary for a time, was beginning to reinforce my depression by treating me as sick. So he backed off to a less intrusive level of caring intervention.

Our family has always pulled together in adversity, and this was no exception. The children and my husband took over many household tasks and chores. With both children in high school, it could have been a time to exercise control over their lives when actually they needed more freedom to grow and take chances. My daughter, Sarah, is the older; I watched her blossom in school as she made her own decisions. My illness had definite downsides, such as Sarah's not feeling free to invite friends over, not knowing my current condition. The children learned to express anger and frustration cautiously because "it might upset Mom." As time passes, these issues continue to surface, and we try to allow a safe place for the expression of those emotions.

I had little stamina, energy, or focus for heavy involvement in the daily details of my children's lives. In retrospect, this was probably healthy for our daughter, Sarah. I had to back off at the time when she needed space. Instead of my parental protectiveness, she learned to rely on her own judgments, to make her own decisions and to live with the consequences, to take the initiative and to follow through. Her character was strengthened, not by instruction or protection from me, but by being tested with the rest of the family. She also became an important person with whom my husband could talk.

Both of our children gained a sensitivity and compassion for persons who are hurting. They learned how to care for me and to pick up the "danger" signals. They knew when to hide the car keys or when to call my husband at work. Often they would just come and sit beside me as I lay in bed. Their love and acceptance were blessings, especially when extended family members found it difficult to communicate support.

FOR SOME REASON WHEN I STARTED TO FEEL better, I got into the sunflower craze. I started collecting sunflower paraphernalia. Soon my family insisted that I confine these "dust collectors" to the kitchen area of our home. My son is a sensitive young man. As he was pondering the sunflower salt and pepper shakers on the table, it struck him that we all have dark centers, like sunflowers, that we try to hide or conceal from others. He wrote a poem for me called "The Sunflower."

There stands a flower in a field.
The flower is different than most others in the field.
This is partly because of its large size,
and partly because of something much deeper.
In the very core of the flower is a dark spot.
The flower worries about its spot,
and so tries to cover its darkness with petals.
The insects notice only the cheery petals on the outside,
and so they flock to the flower
ignoring its dark center.
And time passes.
The flower's roots suck hungrily at the ground
taking in minerals given from rain high above.
The bright yellow sun shines away
allowing the plant to grow further.
With the help of the sun and water,
the plant matures.
The brownish spot changes into scores of seeds.
The warm wind helps carry the seeds away.
And where they land . . .
they bring new life to the world.

ACCEPTANCE

Kübler-Ross suggests that a final stage in the grief process is acceptance. For me, the stage of acceptance was elusive. Seemingly, acceptance does not come to us once and for all, but rather it comes quietly on a daily basis as we are able to open our lives in trust to God's care. Sometimes I was content to just "be" and to abide in the shadow. At other times I fought to gain control of my life. I'd try to analyze what was happening instead of simply accepting, learning, and being open to God's presence in the darkness.

Because I was in and out of acceptance, I was unable to set healthy boundaries for myself. Words or actions of what I now call "toxic people" could easily plunge me into a deep abyss. In my desire to please others, I let people hurt me; I did not assert my own needs. I finally realized that I needed to break off some relationships. Part of my acceptance of the depression was my decision that I was not going to allow these persons to hurt me anymore. Some were family members who found it difficult to deal with past issues.

Many people were well-intentioned in their efforts to help; but their advice or solutions, while appropriate for them, often aroused a negative reaction in me. It seemed that people were more concerned with their own agenda and their own need to "solve" my problem. I did not sense that they truly listened to me or understood me. I perceived their helpful advice as judgment, and even rejection, of my personhood. The pain of depression doesn't require fixing; it requires attentive listening.

I learned that just because I began to experience moments of acceptance didn't mean that other people were at the same place. This was especially true with the church hierarchy. I began to understand why other ministers kept their depression a closely guarded secret. I became aware of meetings being held, without my being included, to determine whether I was able to carry out my ministerial responsibilities. This form of potential rejection while dealing with childhood issues of abandonment and rejection, made me question my vocational decision to leave a teaching career for the church. Suddenly I no longer felt safe in sharing my struggles with the church staff and leaders. The church hierarchy's questioning of my ability to function effectively as a minister intensified the confusing sense of divisiveness I felt inside.

Our church houses many self-help, 12-Step programs. In my anger and following the AA model, I wrote an article entitled, "I Am Susan, and I Am Depressed."[7] In it I wrote that

> depression and other mental illnesses are still widely misunderstood. Instead of being viewed as the treatable illnesses they are, they are talked about in hushed tones and

behind closed doors. Sufferers feel isolated and disconnected from the spiritual community at the time when they need it most. And many are denied access to therapy, medication and social resources that would bring healing and wholeness. Ignorance on the part of others and our own sense of shame and feelings of desolation often prevent us from getting the help we need.

Thankfully, I slowly have learned that no matter what the circumstances, we are not alone in the shadow, even though it often feels that way. Patiently God works in our lives when we are not even aware of it—to bring about the healing and transformation God desires for us. Those moments of grace in the shadow allowed flickers of light to penetrate my darkness.

Break into my confusion, God.

Help me to know who I am
and what I am meant to be.

Guide, uphold and strengthen me,
as I leave behind
the world of limits and labels.

Guide, uphold and strengthen me,
as together we create
a world of infinite possibility.

3 Grace in the Shadow

RACE HAPPENS! THIS INSIGHT CAME TO ME on a particularly difficult morning after a night of little sleep. That morning it took supreme effort on my part to crawl out of bed, shower, dress, and leave for work. As I drove along the freeway, wondering how I was going to make it through the day, I spotted a bumper sticker on the car in front of me. It contained just two words: *Grace Happens*. Taking this as a personal message for me, I walked into the office with a sense of expectancy instead of dread.

I see grace happening in two ways. First, I see redemptive grace, an inbreaking of God's spirit that turns our lives around. We know we will never be quite the same. Second, I see grace in the uniquely Wesleyan doctrine of "prevenient grace." Prevenient means "going before." It is the knowledge that God is quietly at work in our lives whether we are aware of it or not. This grace grounds the practice of infant baptism. When we baptize a child, we affirm that God is already at work in that child's life—before that child can even speak God's name. This optimistic understanding of God's grace is a comfort to those of us who have felt abandoned by God. It affirms that God is at work in our times of deepest darkness and despair—even when we are not aware of that presence.

Grace often happens when we least expect it. As I look back I can see many moments when God's grace broke into my life in unexpected ways. That's what grace is all about. We can't will God's grace or control it. It comes as a gift, often when we are most vulnerable, afraid, hopeless, and alone.

GRACE THROUGH COMMUNION

One such moment occurred when my spiritual director brought me communion during my first stay in the hospital. The sacrament of Communion has always been special to me. This ritual meal connects me to the divine and to other people. The partaking of the Communion elements mysteriously invites God's presence in the innermost part of ourselves. Usually we celebrate Communion before an elaborate altar. But on this occasion there was no altar, or even a table, available in my sparse hospital room. Looking around, we found a trash can. We emptied the trash and turned the can upside down to use as a makeshift altar. I wrote the following about that sacred experience.

Here I am . . . all alone
All alone . . . in a psychiatric hospital.
Events of the past few days
    are a frightening blur.
So here I am, O God, alone in my room
Too ashamed to even ask for visitors.

Yet, my friend comes.
He comes to bring the bread and the cup of life
    in this place, of all places.
An upside-down wastebasket becomes an altar
    and never was any celebration of Holy Communion
    more grace-filled.
An offering . . . an emptying
A letting go . . . a turning over
    of all the waste of my life
    as we huddled together around a wastebasket
    in a hospital room.

O God, your word continues to come to us
in the most unlikely
and unexpected places
. . . and we are not alone anymore.

The literal emptying of that trash can remains a powerful symbol. We all have trash in our lives that we need to empty and release. But some trash is hard to let go of. This is especially true of familiar yet destructive patterns of living or closely held worldviews. As the upside-down wastebasket became an altar, I experienced God's presence even in the difficult process of emptying myself.

The mystery of Holy Communion touched me at other times. Often during my times of deep darkness, I would officiate at the church's vesper Communion service. While sensing my own brokenness, as I put on my vestments, I felt transformed. Those sacred moments connected me to something much greater than myself. I was in "community" even in my isolation; being called out of my personal pain to serve others offered healing.

The sacrament of Communion held special meaning for me on another occasion. It was after my spiritual director moved away, and my pastoral counselor brought Communion to me in the hospital. This time we were in one of the conference rooms, the same room in which I met with my psychiatrist each day. But, again, a transformation occurred. Each of the sacramental items used in the service, which my pastoral counselor shared, held meaning for me. The liturgy was ecumenical, drawing from the many rich traditions of our Christian faith. But I was most touched by the words of Humble Access, words that have been changed in our Protestant liturgies:

> Lord, I am not worthy to receive you,
>   but only say the word and I shall be healed.

I certainly did not feel worthy, which made receiving the Eucharist all the more powerful. My pastoral counselor had baked the bread we used in that service. He asked if I wanted to keep the leftover bread. I "feasted" on that bread with thanksgiving for several days, knowing that I was connected to the larger community even if I did not fully feel that at the time. God's grace was present in that stark hospital room.

GRACE THROUGH CONFIRMATION

My son's confirmation was another profound experience of God's grace. In preparation for his confirmation, I had been reflecting on blessing and how confirmation is really a means by which the church blesses and affirms the youth in their spiritual journey. During this time I also was preparing to lead an upcoming retreat; I chose the subject of blessing as the retreat theme. The process of preparing for that retreat brought up many childhood memories. I felt the loss of not having received "the blessing" from my parents. The deep yearning for parental blessing is rooted in scripture. In the Hebrew culture, blessing was reserved primarily for one special occasion.

The story of Jacob's stealing his father's blessing, which rightfully belonged to the firstborn Esau, has great power because all of us desire a parental blessing. Without that blessing, we continue a lifelong search to find that blessing in some way. Often this search leads to destructive behaviors: We become perfectionists or workaholics. Many of us get caught in a pattern of "pleasing" others, thinking we can earn the blessing that has been denied.

Today we know that giving the blessing need not be a one-time event; we can bless those we love daily. Gary Smalley and John Trent have collaborated on a book entitled *The Gift of the Blessing*, which describes five elements of the blessing. These include meaningful touch, spoken words, expressing high value to persons, picturing a special future for them, and making an active commitment to see that the blessing becomes a reality. Even if we feel we did not receive our family's blessing, God's blessing through our spiritual parentage is secure. Isaiah 43 records these words, "I have called you by name, you are mine. . . . You are precious in my sight, and honored, and I love you." Affirming God's love and adoption of us as sons and daughters is what we do when we baptize or confirm a child into the Christian faith. The community makes a commitment to uphold and care for that person in his or her Christian life.

And so, I was looking forward to my son's confirmation. I told my senior pastor that it felt like a tangible, public way of blessing my son. The pastoral staff would confirm a number of youth that day. While I would participate in the laying on of hands of all the young people, my senior pastor invited me to confirm my son.

My son's confirmation became a time of grace in the shadow for me. As my son knelt before me in front of the congregation, I stepped forward to say the words and to lay hands on his bowed head. I could feel the emotion of the moment, and my throat tightened. As I began to speak, I felt the strong hand of my senior pastor resting on my shoulder. As I confirmed and blessed my son, I felt that I too was receiving a special blessing. Matthew Fox writes, "Blessing involves relationship: one does not bless without investing oneself into the receiver of one's blessing. And one does not receive blessing oblivious of its gracious giver. A blessing spirituality is a relating spirituality."[1]

Real blessings often come to us, I believe, when we are most vulnerable—when we are at our lowest, when we are forced to give up the illusion of control, or when we are feeling most alone and in need of relationship with others and with God. In our times of greatest need, we are most open to the inbreaking of God's love, which affirms a love for us despite our flaws, our wounds, and our weaknesses. On my son's confirmation day, I felt affirmed and loved by God, and my senior pastor's strong hand resting on my shoulder reminded me of God's grace in the dark times.

GRACE THROUGH SYMBOLS

Another time of grace in the shadow came when I told the story of Jesus' birth from Mary's perspective on Christmas morning. I have always appreciated the symbolism surrounding the liturgical seasons of Advent and Christmas. Having given birth, I can relate to the time of waiting, of gestation in the darkness of the womb. During my first pregnancy, I was sick the entire Christmas season; my daughter was born prematurely in early January. I relate to Mary's uncertainty and worry, the strangeness of unfamiliar surroundings. I relate to those first stirrings of life deep inside and the wonder of participating in creation as a child is brought into the world.

Portraying Mary in the midst of my own depression was a healing experience. It brought back strong memories and gave me hope that new life does emerge from the darkness. The events surrounding the birth and the simplicity of it all connected me in some indescribable way with the "sacred ordinary" of daily living. I have not connected in the same way with the violent events that led to Jesus' crucifixion, but I felt close to Mary that Christmas morning.

Perhaps in the midst of my own depression, I sensed the stirrings of new life breaking down the numbness. Mystery surrounds pregnancy and birthing. One must learn to trust in God's timing. The natural processes of birth are not something we can control. After that sermon, I felt a deep connection with the birth narratives and with my own center of mystery.

> *Here I am, Divine Spirit,*
> *living in the center of mystery.*
> *I catch glimpses of brilliant light*
> *breaking in all around.*
> *Yet I am attracted to the darkness*
> *that shields me*
> *that hides me*
> *that keeps me safe.*

I feel yearnings to birth
    the creative spirit within.
Yet I fear the changes
    that new life will bring.
It's hard to understand this place
    this center of mystery.
The light and dark intermingle.
Life and death abide side by side.
It is here that I live the questions
       in my soul,
    knowing that one day
    answers to those questions
    will be birthed
    from this center of mystery.

GRACE THROUGH "PLACE"

Another time of grace in the shadow happened during the season of Lent. I was a participant in the Two Year Academy for Spiritual Formation, which was held at Mercy Retreat Center near San Francisco. The Center grounds were beautiful, and I spent many hours walking by the stream, under the towering oaks, and through the forested areas. The Catholic retreat center had many beautiful stations of the cross. Across from the main entrance, surrounded by a lovely rose garden, was a large white crucifix. A dove's nest was discovered on the shoulder of the dying Christ figure. The sprigs of straw the mother dove had used to make the nest surrounded the head of Christ like a halo. What a tangible, visible sign of new life in our darkest hours this dove's nest became to me!

An image of a cross appeared in a photograph I took at Lake Kanuga in North Carolina. It too became a serendipitous sign of grace to me. Being a native Californian, I was delighted to be at a fall conference in the part of the country that experiences a real change of seasons. I am not a photographer, but I was so intrigued with the ever-changing colors of the lake, the fall leaves, the lily pads, and the rocking chairs on the screened-in porches that I found myself taking many photographs. One of those pictures, taken from the porch of my cabin, shows the mist rising from the lake in the early morning.

Having received many compliments on this photograph, I decided to have it enlarged. When I did, the cross on the other side of the lake, which was not visible in the smaller photo, suddenly appeared. I knew it was there, hidden among the trees and the morning mist, but I had not seen it.

I have since come to appreciate "place" as an important part of our spirituality. I feel rooted in that place, and I return to it often as I look at that photograph. When a person is in the shadow or the mist, it is difficult to believe that one's present unhappiness and despair will ever end. But there it was! The cross in the mist . . . another sign of grace in the shadow.

GRACE THROUGH FAMILY

As mentioned in chapter 2, one of the most painful experiences of my depression was dealing with family members who had difficulty relating to what I was going through. In deciding to suspend some relationships for a period of time, I discovered the grace of letting others become part of my "family." While biological and birth family bonds can be strong, it is possible to invest too much effort in trying to make those relationships be what we would like them to be. Again, one enters a time of loss or grief when we are forced to "let go" of family members' expectations; family members who, for whatever reason, cannot be there for us when we need them. This time of pain can be one of opportunity, a time when we seek out and initiate relationships of mutual vulnerability and trust.

I learned that I could create my own family by allowing those persons I cared about and who cared about me to become "family." A greeting card reminded me that "Friends are the family we choose for ourselves." How true. Many times in my life I have missed having a mother. And, because of my mother's abuse, I found it very difficult to trust women, especially older women. As I have matured, I realized that I had missed out by not having been able to experience close, nurturing relationships with other women. Certain transitions in a woman's life are much easier with a female mentor, guide, and friend.

I am lucky to have found a woman who has become a "surrogate mother" to me. This kind of deep friendship with a woman was new to me, and it took a long time for trust to develop. Being a self-sufficient person, I found it difficult to accept nurture and love from someone else. And again I felt those pangs of loss because I have little remembrance of being nurtured as a child. Our relationship meets both our needs: having no children of her own, she receives satisfaction from both nurturing me and being nurtured by me in return.

I feel fortunate to have found a mother. My husband and children accept her too, realizing how much I needed to be mothered and to receive unconditional love. She continues to teach me things. Her primary blessing to me is as a mentor and role model for she has emerged from her own shadows of darkness from earlier life experiences. She accepts me as I am without negative judgments, guiding and supporting me as I progress in my spiritual journey. She sees in me qualities I have yet to fully appreciate and accept in myself. As I slowly emerge from my depression and regain a sense of joy in life, this special relationship has become yet another gift of grace in the shadow.

Other persons were instruments of God's grace in my darkest time, and they will always be a part of who I am becoming. It took a great deal of time to develop a trusting relationship with my pastoral counselor. In his wisdom, he has continually accepted, respected, and even appreciated wherever I happened to be at the moment. He has always honored my need for withdrawal and solitude and has allowed me to express all my emotions, even when I directed my misplaced anger at him. I always felt that he provided a "safety net"—protection that would not allow me to sink so far as to become a danger to myself. Recognizing my great need for reassurance and stability, he has made himself readily available.

Another important source of grace to me has been my psychiatrist, who has worked persistently to understand my need for healing of mind, spirit, and body. I strongly resisted the use of medication. The inability to find the right medication only increased my reluctance. Having been brought up in the Christian Science faith as a child, some of those core beliefs still linger: that I must fight hard enough or pray hard enough to tough things out. My reluctance to visit the doctor has been superseded by an increased appreciation that God works through doctors and medicine to bring about healing.

But proper medical care is not enough. My wise and patient physician came to understand my need for spiritual grounding. He always takes the time to talk to me about my ministry and to connect me with other persons who are working to blend the fields of psychiatry and spirituality. He encouraged me to share my story with the church community, to expose the stigma of depression. This encouragement was another instance of grace in the shadow.

Grace seldom comes as a profound, single, life-changing event. More often it emerges as a whisper; yet it can carry a person through the next few hours or even days: mornings when I shared bagels and coffee with a friend who listened, offerings of food when I could not begin to plan dinner for the family, phone calls that came at those low moments to lift my spirits and to remind me that I was still connected with others, the memorable sermon or church anthem that touched my soul in a way I cannot describe. Grace happens!

4 Gifts of the Shadow

O Holy God,
    open unto me
        light for my darkness,
        courage for my fear,
        hope for my despair.
O loving God,
    open unto me
        wisdom for my confusion,
        forgiveness for my sins,
        love for my hate.
O God of peace,
    open unto me
        peace for my turmoil,
        joy for my sorrow,
        strength for my weakness.
O generous God,
    open my heart
        to receive all your gifts.
            —Howard Thurman

DEPRESSION IS A POWERFUL TEACHER if we will let it speak. Too often, however, we do not allow depression to share its gifts with us. Thomas Moore in his book *Care of the Soul* states that "If we persist in our modern way of treating depression as an illness to be cured only mechanically and chemically we may lose the gifts of soul that only depression can provide."[1] I recall a reading from twentieth-century preacher Leslie Weatherhead in which he comments that most of us prefer sunlight and happiness. But Weatherhead claims that he learned more in his personal dark times than in the light. He called such learnings "treasures of the darkness," and no one can take these treasures from us. Gifts discovered in the shadow are like "treasures of the darkness" in that they remain a part of us forever.

Gifts are least expected when the veil of darkness suddenly descends upon us. I felt stripped of everything familiar—my patterns of living and especially my ways of experiencing God's presence. I felt lost, not knowing what direction to take; yet, at the same time, I felt helpless and immobilized to move in any direction. Depression is a bewildering experience and certainly not a time to recognize or appreciate God's hidden work in our lives. Sandra Cronk in *Dark Night Journey* sees the dark night as time for "an intensive re-patterning of our whole being."[2] This drastic transformation does not occur without deep emotional pain.

The more I struggled to regain my bearings and sense of control, the deeper I descended into the darkness. Cronk goes on to say that,

> Letting go of the need to control our spiritual path is especially helpful in the dark night because in these times we do not choose a path. We experience the path as given. Walking in trust, along the path that is given, is our way of saying yes to God.[3]

When you suddenly find yourself alone and without direction, walking this path requires a trust that is difficult to come by. I tried to flee the emptiness in search of meaning; but the harder I tried to control my emotional and spiritual life and tried to control and manipulate God, the more desolate I felt.

I learned that the darkness does not yield because we will it to do so. Rather, it becomes more intense. I was in unfamiliar territory; my predominant emotion was fear. My old patterns of behavior no longer worked, and I lost a sense of my own identity. I experienced only the void of God's absence, and a deep emptiness surrounded me.

The gifts of the shadow do not yield themselves easily. They begin to emerge from the depths only as we are willing to let go and be present to the darkness. I have found strength and solace in the many who have traveled this dark path before me. I found myself clinging to their words of consolation and hope. One particular prayer from Thomas Merton has been especially helpful.

> I have no idea where I am going. I do not see the road ahead of me. I cannot know for certain where it will end. Nor do I really know myself, and the fact that I think I am following your will does not mean that I am actually doing so. But I believe that the desire to please you does in fact please you. And I hope I have that desire in all that I am doing. I hope that I will never do anything apart from that desire. And I know that if I do this you will lead me by the right road, though I may know nothing about it. Therefore I will trust you always though I may seem to be lost and in the shadow of death. I will not fear, for you are ever with me, and you will never leave me to face my perils alone.[4]

I often felt "lost and in the shadow of death." My fears were so strong that for a long time I was numb, unable to move in the darkness. Gradually, with the encouragement and patience of my pastoral counselor, I was able to find the courage to begin to grope around in the darkness. Through this painstaking exploration of the hidden places of my soul, I began to discover that my depression was an unasked-for opportunity to explore the depths of my inner self. Deepak Chopra says, "When you embrace and become intimate with your Shadow Self, you get in touch with the totality of your Being. In that totality lies wholeness. You are holy and you are healed."

In this chapter, I will share some of the "gifts of soul" and "treasures of darkness" that I have uncovered as I have stumbled along in the shadow of death.

WHEN PERSONS FIND themselves in the shadow, one immediate reaction is that of fear, accompanied by the desire to distance themselves from the darkness. Our impulse is to run, to hide, to flee the darkness. But the dark nights of our souls—whether caused by illness, crisis, or some unknown origin—can be pathways to transformation and healing, opportunities for personal growth, and the means of becoming new persons in Christ.

The first treasure of darkness is the gift of vulnerability, a gift that encompasses all the other gifts. I see vulnerability's unfolding in three ways. First, there is vulnerability to God. Second, there is an admission of one's own vulnerability. And third, we build enough trust to make ourselves vulnerable to others.

VULNERABILITY TO GOD

For me, becoming vulnerable to God meant that I had to relinquish many of my childhood conceptions of God. I grew up believing in God's omnipotence; yet God did not protect me from the suffering of my childhood or from my mother's wrath. God did not heal my mother of cancer, even though I prayed in earnest. God was absent in my deepest depression when I needed God's presence the most.

I was angry. I was angry at God for not "fixing" things. I desired the powerful God of my upbringing, a God who could step in to make things right. I strongly identified with Job and the writers of the Psalms. I found myself in prayer, lashing out at God for the anguish and despair I was feeling. I lashed out at God for leaving me utterly alone in my misery. I lashed out at God for not saving me from my time of trial.

I am coming to understand God's power in a new way. I am coming to understand God as a vulnerable God who suffers with us in our painful times. Jesus at Golgotha epitomizes this vulnerable God. This understanding helped me identify with Jesus' words in the garden of Gethsemane: "My God, my God, why have you forsaken me?" I realized that Jesus too felt utterly abandoned and alone—by his friends and by God. And yet, he is able to say also, "My Father, if it is possible, let this cup pass from me; yet not what I want but what you want" (Matt. 26:39). Later Jesus says, "Father, into your hands I commend my spirit" (Luke 23:46). In that relinquishment, Jesus found that he was not alone.

Like most people, I struggle between my desire to trust and my need for security and control. Our society does not make it easy to trust anyone or any institution. The greater my fear, the more I try to control those things in my life over which I think I have some control. The greater my fear, the more I try to play it "safe." The greater my fear, the more trust seems like a distant and far-off ideal. I am unable to trust others, and I am certainly far from putting my trust in God. It is difficult to trust God when you cannot see the path before you or any glimmer of light in the darkness.

But there comes a time when we find ourselves utterly helpless, vulnerable, and weak; only then are we able to rely on God. How sad that many of us cannot abide in that state of trust. But in my experience, crisis and its ensuing vulnerability finally allow us to open ourselves to God's presence.

ADMISSION OF ONE'S VULNERABILITY

Becoming vulnerable to God is a first step. But we must still admit our vulnerability to ourselves. This involves coming to terms with our own suffering. It means coming to terms with our own mortality. And it involves allowing the events of life and the actions of others to affect us. It is a letting down of the barriers we may have taken years to carefully construct—the barriers that have served us well in the past and in which we have a vested interest in preserving for our personal security.

One of my favorite Bible stories tells of a person coming to terms with her suffering and vulnerability. Mark 5:21-34 records the story of the woman with the uncontrollable hemorrhage. We don't know much about this unnamed woman. We do know that she had used all the human resources available to be healed of the bleeding, and they had all proved insufficient. She had spent all her money on unsuccessful medical treatments. The Gospel writer tells us this. What the Gospel writer doesn't tell us—but what we know from the culture of that time—is that the hemorrhage rendered her ritually impure. The cleanliness laws were very clear for men and for women. The primary causes of impurity and uncleanness were childbirth; leprosy and other diseases of the skin; dead bodies of certain animals but especially human corpses and their blood; and the discharge of bodily fluids, particularly the flow of blood.

Something in this woman caused her to overcome her fear of the purity laws and take the risk of being healed, of being made whole. This is a wonderful example of how many of us act today. We have this great need to find the answers ourselves,until we are spent—physically, financially, and emotionally. Finally we have no choice but to reach out and touch that which is greater than ourselves.

Not only did this woman defy the purity laws, but she had the audacity to touch the most sacred part of Jesus' clothing—the fringe on his cloak or outer garment. Jewish men wore cloaks that had a cord or thread, which ended in a kind of tassel sewn on at the four corners of the garment. Both Numbers and Deuteronomy indicate that the tassels were to be worn on the outer garment where they were most conspicuous. They were a sacred part of a man's clothing, a sacred part of his identity as a Jew. So it was even more bold and even more of a taboo that this unclean woman would reach out and touch the fringe of Jesus' cloak.

The stories of Jesus' power had stirred the woman's faith: *If I but touch his clothes*, she thought, *I will be made well*. Slowly she moved into the throbbing mass and edged forward, positioning herself close enough to barely touch Jesus' clothes. And Jesus immediately sensed that power had gone from him—another example of divine vulnerability. Jesus turned to the crowd and said, "Who touched my clothes?" To the disciples, it was a foolish question. They said, "You see the crowd pressing in on you; how can you say, 'Who touched me?'" As Jesus looked around, the woman in fear and trembling fell down before him and told him the whole truth. In the telling, she discovered a way to new life. And Jesus gave her a blessing of peace and a benediction of restored health: "Daughter, your faith has made you well; go in peace, and be healed of your disease."

I find it remarkable that while this woman was able to admit her vulnerability and reach out in trust that Jesus could heal her, she still approached Jesus with fear and trembling. Admitting one's vulnerability is not a one-time event! Most of us take a step forward in trust, only to retreat in fear to the security and safety of the familiar. It takes time to learn to trust, especially when that trust has been broken in our past. It is difficult to let go of our need for control; but when we do, we find healing and a new way of living.

VULNERABILITY TO OTHERS

Another big step in recognizing our vulnerability is trusting enough to make ourselves vulnerable to others. The importance of community is vital here. We do not live in isolation, and we truly cannot receive healing and wholeness without community. Communities based on mutual vulnerability encourage healing. Twelve-Step programs' popularity and success are a powerful testimony to mutual vulnerability.

I spent most of my time in the shadow carefully guarding my vulnerability from others—especially from the church. But there came a point when I could no longer carry the burden of silence. I relate my experiences of dealing with the church community in the chapter "Emerging from the Shadow." But subtle changes began to occur before my public admission of depression. Almost without knowing it, I began modeling a style of vulnerability in my church activities. People noticed a change in the tone of my pastoral prayers, and my counseling skills were enhanced. I no longer felt that I was there to "fix" people's problems or to offer textbook solutions. I was there simply as a presence and a reminder of God's grace and presence to others.

In my own weakness, I often doubted my ability to minister. But I gradually discovered that real power does not reside in authority. Real power comes in humility, in recognizing one's own weakness, and in vulnerability. When we are able to admit our vulnerabilities to God, to ourselves, and to the community, God graces us with a power to help others. We become "wounded healers"; we can share with others the gifts of grace and healing we have received. As Henri Nouwen stated in his book *The Wounded Healer*, we are called as Christians "to make our painful and joyful experiences available as sources of clarification and understanding."[5] Often our wounded places become wellsprings of sharing with others. Wounds become signs of hope.

I think of Jesus after the Resurrection. When the risen Christ first appeared to the disciples in the Upper Room, Thomas was not among them. Upon hearing the news, Thomas said he would not believe without seeing the marks of the nails. What did Jesus do? He showed Thomas his wounds. Even the risen Christ came to new life with scars, wounds, and marks of his struggle in the darkness. In sign language for the hearing impaired, the sign for *Jesus* is to point with the third finger of one hand to the palm of the other and vice versa. The risen Christ is identified by the nail scars in his hands. The marks of his struggle in the darkness remain and become the identifying marks of God's goodness and love.

It has taken time to recognize and acknowledge my continuing vulnerability. Those of us who have been to the depths always fear that something will cause us to plummet again into that deep darkness. The times I have tried to fight off the fear of my vulnerability have been the times when my fear has returned in full force. Instead of fighting vulnerability, I am learning to accept it and incorporate it into the person I am becoming.

Acceptance of my vulnerability has greatly impacted my approach to pastoral counseling. I am able to be authentically present to the suffering of a hurting person in a way I never could before my depression. I am not the authority, the holder of advice or easy solutions gleaned from my readings. I am not merely a good listener. Rather, when appropriate, I find myself sharing my own painful experiences and some of what I have learned in the shadow. I begin each session with a prayer before the parishioner ever enters my office, acknowledging my own limitations and praying for God's spirit to guide the session. And I always close my sessions with a prayer that the person would be open to God's grace working in his or her situation. I am humbled by entering another's sacred space, and I always acknowledge that God is the Great Healer.

The gift of vulnerability does not come easily, but it is a great treasure. While struggling with issues of change, fear, and trust, I wrote about "The Child Within" who, like the woman with the hemorrhage, seeks new life.

> *Parent God, the little child within*
> *is stirring in the darkness.*
> *The little child is stretching*
> *and pushing*
> *ever so gently*
> *against the protective womb.*

The little child is also frightened, God.
She wants to trust,
  but past experience
  has sent her fleeing
  to the safety of this place.

She has such strong needs . . .
  to be held tightly and securely
  to be cared for and fussed over
  to be nurtured and loved
  to be accepted just as she is.
The little child has tried before
  to break forth into the light.
But guilt, ridicule, and, oh, so much fear
  have held her back.

God of Darkness and God of Light,
  surround this child
  with your healing presence.
Encircle her with your grace and love.
Hold her hand tightly,
  that she might find the courage and strength
  to seek the new freedom and the new life
  she desires so.

The Gift of Discovering One's Authentic Self

I PICTURE MYSELF CROUCHED on an old rope bridge suspended between two cliffs, tightly clutching the tattered ropes. I am terrified of heights. On the cliff to my left are those persons in my past who beckon me to come "home." I'm not sure who or what is on the cliff to the right. I do know it is a slick wall of rock; the only way out is to be pulled up by a rope.

Below me is a murky pool of unidentified origin or description. I call it "sludge." It is dark and foreboding. Occasionally my fears have emerged from the sludge, and I have been able to identify and name them. When this occurs, I am still fearful but I know what I am dealing with. Other times I am too afraid even to look down. I was often immobilized—unable to move in any direction.

This recurring and haunting image has appeared in various forms in my dreams and has found a place in my scribblings and drawings. The primary feeling that surfaces from this image is one of disconnection—disconnection from self, not knowing who my "self" really is. This disorientation is terrifying; I feel cut off from all the "selves" and patterns that have served me for so many years. Each time I gain courage to try a new behavior, a backlash of old messages from the left side of the bank tells me I will fail. Then once again, I am unable to move in any direction, and I sit there in terror in the middle of that fragile bridge.

I have come to realize that my experience mirrors the discontinuity between our projected self (often referred to as our ego) and our authentic God-given self. Once again I find meaning in the Psalms. Psalm 139 declares that God "formed my inward parts; you knit me together in my mother's womb. I praise you, for I am fearfully and wonderfully made. Wonderful are your works" (vss. 13-14). Most of the time I do not feel "wonderfully made." God created us to be whole persons, but we have strayed from God's purposes and have forgotten who we are. Thus, a feeling of disconnectedness marks our lives, a sense of not knowing where we belong.

The church and our Western culture have contributed to this disconnectedness in many ways. Paul, in his writings, elevates the way of the spirit over the ways of our mortal bodies. In Romans 8 Paul writes, "To set the mind on the flesh is death, but to set the mind on the Spirit is life and peace. For this reason the mind that is set on the flesh is hostile to God; it does not submit to God's law—indeed it cannot, and those who are in the flesh cannot please God" (vss. 6-8). In Galatians 5:17, Paul further states, "For what the flesh desires is opposed to the Spirit, and what the Spirit desires is opposed to the flesh; for these are opposed to each other."

Paul reflected the dualistic Greek thought of his day, which focused on the split between the spirit and nature. The early church fostered discussion around this thought as it formulated, debated, wrote, and revised its creeds. Celibacy and other forms of renunciation, such as fasting, were forms of rejecting the physical world in an attempt to raise oneself above this world to some form of idealized spirituality. The age of Enlightenment (a philosophic movement of the eighteenth century, which emphasized rationalism) further separated human beings into body and mind. While this separation led to significant scientific advances, we lost the sense of mystery, awe, and wonder about ourselves and about our relationship to the natural world.

REUNITE MIND, BODY, AND SPIRIT

More recent times have brought forth efforts to reunite mind, body, and spirit. The renewed emphasis on healing offers integration of oneself rather than division. Persons such as John A. Sanford, Gerald May, Bill Moyers, Deepak Chopra, and Thomas Moore, to name a few, are combining the truths of psychology with those of spirituality. A major advance in psychiatry occurred with the publication of the Diagnostic and Statistical Manual of Mental Disorders in 1994. The fourth edition of the DSM-IV, published by the American Psychiatric Association, recognized for the first time that a "religious or spiritual problem" may affect a person's mental health. In diagnoses, "This category can be used when the focus of clinical attention is a religious or spiritual problem."[6]

Dr. Howard Clinebell, well-known author in the field of pastoral counseling, in his recent book *Well Being* provides a wonderful guide for helping people achieve the wholeness we all desire, and which God desires for us. Clinebell states that

> There *is* a precious treasure within you waiting to be discovered and used. It is the treasure of your potentialities—your possibilities for a healthier, more alive, more fulfilled, productive, and love-energized life.[7]

Dr. Clinebell goes on to suggest ways of enriching seven dimensions of our lives: mind, body, spirit, love, work, play, and earth. Clearly, many professionals are discovering that you cannot merely treat the body with chemicals and the mind with therapies of various types. It is recognized that an illness of any type may be the catalyst to a person's discovering his or her authentic self.

Discovering the treasure of oneself in the shadow is not an easy process. At first I wanted to throw out and even destroy all that I was, seeing no value in who I perceived Susan to be. Slowly I came to understand that there was some good in Susan; indeed, some parts were "wonderfully made." But those parts were hidden in the sludge under the bridge, and it was difficult to discover the treasure. I found it much easier to identify and name all the things I did not like about myself and then to "beat myself up" for who I thought I was. One of the keys to learning to love oneself is to get to know oneself. That takes time and attention.

One does not achieve wholeness by cutting off portions of oneself but by integrating these contrary parts into a new creation. We undertake a gradual process of integrating those false or counterfeit selves into our emerging true self. Only then are we truly grounded in ourselves, yet connected to all.

HONOR SELF

One of the keys to discovering my authentic self was Jesus' words, "Love your neighbor as yourself." All my life I've tried to practice loving and reaching out to my neighbor. But I ignored the second part of Jesus' commandment: We are to love ourselves first! I perceived that to be an impossible task. In the depths of my depression, I hated myself.

Honoring oneself often requires one to reevaluate and reprioritize use of time. Too many of us suffer from burnout. We need down time. The scriptures recognize this need for times of rest and renewal. This time of re-creation is the meaning behind the word *Sabbath*. Attending church for an hour on Sunday morning is not sufficient. The need to rediscover the Sabbath as a time of rest and renewal is evident, but accomplishing this in our fast-paced world is anything but easy. I'm as guilty as the next person for using my day off to catch up on office work,household chores, grocery shopping, laundry, and other errands.

RECLAIM SABBATH TIME

I'm seeking to reclaim Sabbath time in my life. I believe we first need to honestly examine how we spend the bulk of our time. Consider recording all you do in a week's time. Then list those activities that are most meaningful to you, that give you pleasure, and that nurture your soul. Compare the two lists to see if you are spending time on those values and priorities that are most important to you. This simple exercise may suggest some areas in your life where you need to make adjustments.

I recommend making room for daily Sabbath time. It can be as simple as changing your perspective as you begin to recognize the presence of God in the activities of daily life. All of life is sacred, and we are the recipients of God's abundant grace each day. We need to recognize and celebrate God's presence with us in the midst of our busy lives.

Being attentive to God's presence includes taking time throughout the day to stretch, walk and read for pleasure, or to simply close your eyes and rest quietly in God's presence. When I am particularly stressed, I find that a few minutes spent working in my garden helps me reconnect to God's created world. I recently purchased a pillow as a gift to myself, which says, "Gardening grows the spirit."

At night we need a deep, recuperative sleep as a time of totally letting go of control so the mind can do its work, straightening out jumbled messages received during the day. This deep sleep is important for dreaming, which is another way the mind works to relieve the day's tensions.

Besides taking time to relax daily, I have found that I need minivacations—maybe lasting only five minutes—every day throughout the week. The change of pace can be anything that allows you to pay attention to something that you find pleasurable. At first I felt guilty about scheduling time for myself. But I discovered that I am a much happier wife, mother, and minister if I feel centered. I signed up for an occasional massage, which was initially very difficult, since I associated touch with physical abuse. But I have discovered the healing power of touch.

Each person has his or her own rhythm. I have discovered that I need to take a few days away every three or four months in order to recreate myself and to allow myself time for openness to God's direction. Times of "doing nothing," times spent on creative projects, times of Sabbath rest and renewal, and periods of waiting can be times when we are particularly open to the sacred in ordinary, everyday life. When not consumed by our own agendas, the holy may surprise us.

All of this relates to our attitudes and feelings about time;

how we structure it and give ourselves permission to make changes that will enhance our spiritual life as well as our physical and mental well-being. Time is a gift from God, and time management is indeed a spiritual discipline necessary for a healthy, whole, and holy life. All of us need to find ways to create sacred space in our lives that we might be graced by "godly moments."

LISTEN

Another way to discover who I really am is to begin to listen. I started journaling almost daily when I first realized that my life was changing in ways I could not understand. Journal writing need not be an additional chore that you must diligently practice. Simply writing when you feel moved to write can help you discern the Spirit's movement in your life. Looking back over four years of my writings, I can see God's "prevenient grace" at work—at work in my life, even when I was unaware of its presence. God was with me in the darkest times as Psalm 139:7-12 promises:

> Where can I go from your spirit?
>   Or where can I flee from your presence?
> If I ascend to heaven, you are there;
>   if I make my bed in Sheol, you are there.
> If I take the wings of the morning
>   and settle at the farthest limits of the sea,
> even there your hand shall lead me,
>   and your right hand shall hold me fast.
> If I say, "Surely the darkness shall cover me,
>   and the light around me become night,"
> even the darkness is not dark to you;
>   the night is as bright as the day,
>   for darkness is as light to you.

I am also learning to listen to myself through dreams and images, such as the recurring dream of the suspension bridge. I record my dreams or dream fragments in my journal. Dreams symbolically represent the state of the soul. Often they mean nothing to me at the time; but as I go back and read over my journal, I find a richness of symbolism and meaning that I had previously missed.

SYMBOLIZE

Symbols have also helped as I have sought to find my way through the shadows. Symbols differ from signs. Signs point to something that is known; symbols point the way to the unknown, to an understanding of oneself at a deeper level.

I have a wonderful picture in my office entitled "Portals." It depicts two dark doors opening only slightly. Outside the portals is a hint of blended, muted colors contrasting the darkness of the massive doors. There is no definition to this space outside the doors.

The picture speaks to me as I sit at my desk; it is on the wall directly opposite my desk. Looking at the picture, I sometimes feel a part of it. Some days I find that I need to stay on this side of the doors, protected somehow by their dark massive presence. Other days I am willing to venture out into the unknown, just a little. There I find a beckoning beauty in the undefined, soft colors. But what lies beyond the doors is still an unknown. If I get scared, I can always run back to the safety of the protective dark doors. I am finding that, as my healing progresses, I am able to stay outside those doors for longer periods of time. I realize that my depression is lifting when I am able to venture outside those doors and fully enjoy life again.

Each person has to find symbols that speak to him or her. The lion cub Simba in the movie *The Lion King* became an important part of my journey. My journey paralleled that of Simba's in his quest to become his authentic self. Simba and his friend enter the forbidden "shadowy place" that lays beyond the boundary of the Prideland. His father saves him from certain death by the hyenas. To me, the hyenas represent the fearful and hidden things lurking in the shadows. Simba's uncle Scar then leads Simba and his father into "the valley of the shadow of death" and plans to have them killed by a stampede. Scar kills Simba's father but blames the death on the young lion. Scar tells Simba to "run away and never return." Simba does run away, overwhelmed with the guilt of responsibility for his father's death.

I too lived in guilt for things done, which I believed to be my fault. I now know that I did the best I could at the time, given my age and my circumstances. Maya Angelou, author and poet, put it so well in the words I recall from a recent television interview: "You did what you had to do and when you knew better, you did better."

The prodigal Simba did what he had to do by making a new life, free of any responsibilities. But the baboon "witch doctor" discovers Simba and reminds the lion that he cannot change the past and that it is time for Simba to discover who he is. The spirit of his dead father then appears and tells Simba, "You have forgotten who you are. Look inside yourself, Simba. You are more than what you have become. You must take your place in the circle of life. Remember who you are."

Those are powerful words, reminiscent of our baptism: *Remember who you are.* Out of fear, guilt, or past regrets, many of us have become less than what God intends for us. But our baptism affirms us as God's children. We are loved and accepted regardless of our past mistakes and regrets. To fully remember who and whose we are often requires that we, like Simba, enter into our own shadows. And like Simba, the encouragement of others helps us move out of those shadows to claim our true identity. I have my own stuffed baby Simba, which reminds me that I am still becoming who God has already created me to be. Like Simba, I know that the past can hurt, but we may choose to run from it or to learn from it.

A sculpture in my backyard, which I can see as I look out my kitchen window, also holds symbolic meaning for me. It is of a girl with her eyes lifted to the sky. Her cupped hands hold a bird. The artist titled the sculpture "Joy." When I experience no joy in my own life, this symbol reminds me that the hope of joy is a constant, no matter how I may be feeling at the moment.

Symbols also have become important in creating my own sacred space. I have created such a space in my home. Its fountain represents the "living water." I placed various other symbols around the fountain on the small round table. Stones from a local beach have served as an outlet for my creative and spiritual expression. I have drawn a representative animal from the Native American tradition on each stone. Each animal represents a gift I feel I need. The bear represents power and direction; the squirrel, trust; the seagull, grace and adaptability; the deer, love and gentleness; the wolf, perseverance and protector; the caribou, self-esteem; and, most important, the eagle represents the Divine Spirit. A clay dove and a stone turtle also rest beside the fountain. The dove reminds me of the inner peace I seek in my life, and the turtle lets me know that it is my choice whether or not to come out of the shell.

Each of these ways of honoring myself and listening to my inner self has been a path in my journey to discover who I am. I'm reminded of Jesus' parable of the treasure hidden in the field. That treasure, symbolizing the kingdom of God, is of such supreme value, that when someone stumbles across it and recognizes it, the person sells everything to own the treasure. I have struggled to discover the treasure in the field of my soul. Often I have felt a need to work harder in therapy, and I have become impatient with where I am. Discovering one's authentic self ultimately involves cooperation and openness to the grace of God, who has placed the treasure deep in the soul, awaiting discovery.

So often, Divine One
>*the tasks before me*
>*feel overwhelming and impossible.*
>*The expectations of others weigh heavy*
>*upon my shoulders.*

At times like these,
>*I think I need to do something*
>*to invest more time and effort*
>*to pray longer and harder*
>*to embark on a journey*
>*in search of the Kingdom.*

When I am too tired to "do" anymore
>*when I am content just to "be"*
>*when I stop long enough to rest*
>*when I am finally ready to give up*
I find myself sitting on a treasure
>*You have hidden in a field*
>*waiting for me to discover.*

When I lift the treasure
>*from its hiding place,*
>*I find that You have*
>*graced me with adequacy*
>*for all that lies ahead.*

The Gift of Patience within a Process

WHEN OUR CHILDREN were younger, we would often take car trips. I remember the long rides and the frequent inquiries from our restless young riders, "When are we going to get there?" "How much longer?" We would give an estimated time of arrival and brace ourselves for the repeated questions five minutes later. Our secret hope, of course, was that they would fall asleep until we reached our destination. Thankfully those family trips had an end, a time of arrival.

Unlike those family trips, depression has no predictable time of arrival, no time when one says the depression has ended, and total healing has taken place. So, like my children, I frequently ask God, "How much longer?"

A sign in my son's room reads, "Be patient. God is not finished with me yet." God is not finished with any of us. I think many of us feel the inevitable tension between God's timing and our timing. That tension permeates the Bible and our Christian tradition. How do we learn to abide in the between time with a sense of expectancy that God's kingdom will come? Like Abraham and Sarah and many other biblical figures, we are often called to go on a journey. Many times we do not know where we are going or when we have arrived.

One of the most frightening feelings that accompanies depression is the sense that it will never end. Hopelessness and emptiness are part of every minute of every day. My prayers reflected my real sense of having been abandoned by God in the time of my greatest need. The waiting for a sign of hope is interminable. The temptation is to give in to the despair and to "shut down." In doing so, we fail to recognize God's presence in our daily lives.

WAITING ON GOD

Most of us experience despair at some time at our sense of a silent God. Many of the Psalms relate the frustration and distress of waiting for God to save us. This sense of being abandoned and forgotten by God is quite real and personal in Psalm 22:1-2. The psalmist cries out, "My God, my God, why have you forsaken me? Why are you so far from helping me, from the words of my groaning? O my God, I cry by day, but you do not answer; and by night, but find no rest."

Instead of closing down, I have discovered the importance of using these dark times as productively as possible. Slowly I am learning to think of even the darkest moments as a gift of the shadow. It involves reclaiming the spiritual discipline of waiting patiently on God. Patient waiting does not mean that we do nothing; it is not the absence of action. To practice patient waiting is to acknowledge and accept where we happen to be at any given time. The more I tried to be somewhere other than where I was, the more disconnected I became. I was trying to control my illness, wishing and hoping that my life was different. This need to control often involved prayers telling God what to do to improve my plight.

I still have trouble with patient waiting. But when I can abide in my present and live in trust that God is at work in my life, I find myself more open to God's inbreaking grace. I am more integrated than disconnected. When I can live in trust that new life and new beginnings may come in ways I never expected, then I am actively present and expectant that things may happen beyond my wildest imagination. Again I relate to Mary. No one expected, least of all Mary, that God would choose to give the gift of love to all humanity through a poor, peasant girl and a vulnerable baby.

I am learning that God's presence is in the waiting and the wondering, in the ponderings of my heart. Through patient waiting, we discover God's activity in the process of our current situation. Often that process is hidden, but we receive clues to these reminders of God's presence. Patient waiting requires living in expectancy and the willingness to be surprised.

I have led a women's spirituality group using Macrina Wiederkehr's book *A Tree Full of Angels*. Her book reminded me that all of life is sacred, even when we are living in the shadow. We feel alone and abandoned, and we desire a presence of some sort. Wiederkehr says,

> Presence is what we are all starving for. Real presence! We are too busy to be present, too blind to see the nourishment and salvation in the crumbs of life, the experiences of each moment. Yet the secret of life is this: *There are no leftovers!*
>
> There is nothing—no thing, no person, no experience, no thought, no joy or pain—that cannot be harvested and used for nourishment on our journey to God.[8]

This desire for real presence is universal; it is not just for those who live with depression. Wiederkehr's insight—that on our journey to God we can harvest even our pain—gave me comfort. In our times of patient waiting, our awareness of God's presence allows us to discover our salvation in the crumbs of our lives.

Over the years of my depression, I have had many dreams about birthing. They always vary, but recording those dreams made me more aware of the process of growth. When I looked back at each "crumb," I could see God at work. In my initial dreams, the baby was born dead. Later I had a dream in which the baby was born and looked perfectly normal to everyone else. To me it had no form, and I wanted to smother it. Subsequent dreams involved babies born too early, much like my own two children. They were not ready to leave the safety and security of the womb, and I was not yet ready to leave the safety of the wall I had built to protect myself.

We often do not see the growth that occurs within. We must

learn to be patient and trust the process, believing that within the stillness and the darkness, life will be born anew.

One of the most helpful books in my journey has been *When the Heart Waits* by Sue Monk Kidd. I received the book just prior to my first hospitalization. My concentration was poor, but each day I would read a small portion of the book. It was one of those times when I knew that a book had been written just for me!

Sue Monk Kidd has a wonderful image in her book. She calls it the "spiritual art of cocooning." Like the caterpillar undergoing transformation in the cocoon, it takes time. The process cannot be rushed. Sue Monk Kidd writes,

> The fullness of one's soul evolves slowly. We're asked to go within to gestate the newness God is trying to form; we're asked to collaborate with grace. . .
>
> . . . Spirit needs a container to pour itself into. Grace needs an arena in which to incarnate. [9]

I found it difficult to allow my darkness to be an open, receptive container for God's grace. I wasn't acknowledging that the shadow of God's wings covered my darkness, that God was working in the darkness to bring wholeness and healing.

God's love existed before I experienced any human rejection and will endure beyond any rejections I may experience in the future. Patient waiting and stillness create that space for God's grace. But one also becomes more vulnerable. We are vulnerable because we are caught in that uncomfortable in-between time. We know we are changing, but we cannot yet see the end product. What we are to be, we are becoming. And so we trust that there is meaning and direction in our lives beyond the emptiness and isolation we may be experiencing. It is a fearful place to be because it involves great trust in what is not yet known to us. It is a time when we need to be "held" by others who can reassure us that everything will be all right. It was a time when I made many calls to my pastoral counselor. Even as

I grew stronger, I became more vulnerable to the messages of my past. I knew I couldn't go back, but neither could I hurry the birth of my authentic self.

I recall the season of Lent during the second year of my depression. I decided that the depression had gone on long enough and that this year Easter was going to be my resurrection too. But as Easter approached, it was not time. I wrote the following:

I'm not ready for Easter, Lord.
I'm still living in the shadow of the cross.
The weight of the anxieties I carry
*   is still heavy on my back.*
Yet I've pulled away from those persons
*   who could help me carry the load.*
I cry out, "My God, my God,
*   why have you forsaken me?"*
Yet I know it is I
*   who have turned away*
*   denied you*
*   rejected you.*

In the shadow of the cross,
*   I live in paradox.*
I want your light,
*   but find comfort in darkness.*
I want to trust,
*   but doubts overcome me.*
I want to die with you,
*   but new life frightens me.*

The crowds have gone.
Some have even discovered
*   the mystery of the empty tomb,*
*   while I remain here alone,*
*   in the shadow of the cross.*

In this solitude,
   I seek your presence.
In this silence,
   I listen
   for the whisper of your grace.
Remember this child, O God,
   living in the shadow of the cross.

The Gift of Living with Paradox

THE DICTIONARY DESCRIBES paradox as "something inconsistent with common experience or having contradictory qualities." One of the synonyms given for paradox is "mystery," or "that which cannot be explained." Our culture thrives on instant gratification; living with paradox and mystery does not come easily to us. We prefer the easy answers. Living with paradox does not imply that we try to achieve a perfect balance, for balance is not a static point. It is a dance between two polarities. We resist the dance. We resist struggling with issues that offer no easy answers.

Depression can bring with it the gift of learning to live with paradox. But this gift does not come easily to the person experiencing depression. One of the foremost characteristics of depression is seeing things as either black or white. Professionals who work in the field call it "all or nothing thinking."

PARADOX OF GOOD AND EVIL

I struggle with a number of issues focusing on paradox and mystery. One is acceptance of the intermingling of the darkness and the light and learning to appreciate the areas of gray. Slowly I am learning to embrace those parts of myself that I have rejected or pushed into the shadow of my subconscious self because of my own fear. Gradually I am learning the importance of confronting those fears and accepting those parts of myself that I had rejected.

The paradox lies in the fact that the parts of ourselves that we have buried in the shadow of the subconscious are essential to our becoming integrated, whole persons. When brought into the light, those qualities we have rejected are transformed by God's grace. They, in turn, strengthen our whole personality.

Often we resist that which can bring healing and salvation. We are split between what we consciously know to be true and what lies in our subconscious. Living in this tension is difficult because often contradictory parts of ourselves are struggling for control, and we cannot consciously, by our own will, bring these conflicting parts together. We cannot save ourselves. Rather, the emergence of the whole self is a process dependent on God's grace.

Several scripture passages refer to losing one's life in order to find it. In Matthew 10:39, Jesus says "Those who find their life will lose it, and those who lose their life for my sake will find it." I think Jesus is reminding us that we cannot save ourselves. To lose one's life is to give up the illusion of control and to become vulnerable. Healing of mind, body, and spirit is hard work—and scary. Seemingly contradictory dynamics are at work. It is difficult to know when to use our intellect, resource-fulness, and yearning to be made whole—to "do" something. It is just as hard to know when to let go, to surrender, to just "be." The paradox is that healing is both work and no work; it is not we who do the healing. We can encourage healing and create an environment for it, but we cannot bring about healing by our-selves. We are part of a process, but always God is the Great Physician.

In many ways healing comes about through faith when we surrender to God. Jean Blomquist has written the following in the journal *Weavings*:

> Surrender is not so much a giving up as it is an *opening* up. It is a dynamic living and striving in the face of the unknown. When we surrender in faith, we enter into the

power of God, into the realm of all possibility. We open ourselves to new perspectives, thoughts and dimensions of life yet to be explored.[10]

The struggle between conflicting emotions in my feelings toward my mother has been an example of my moving from all-or-nothing feelings to a gradual acceptance of the contradictory parts of my mother's personality. For years I held on to the illusion that my mother was the perfect, loving mother. When the bubble burst and I acknowledged the abuse, I did an about-face and decided that my mother was all bad. Yet I tried to reconcile the love I still felt for my mother by making excuses for her behavior.

I finally had to come to that gray place somewhere in between. I was able to recognize the good while still accepting that my mother—like all of us—had her faults, weaknesses, and failures. She made some serious mistakes and undoubtedly struggled with a number of issues in her life. But my coming to accept that each of us has good qualities as well as faults helped me to escape my all-or-nothing thinking. I no longer make excuses for her behavior, and my anger has been transformed primarily by my understanding that she too did the best she could under the circumstances.

PARADOX OF THE KNOWN AND THE UNKNOWN

I am also learning to live in the paradox between the known and the unknown. I have so many questions of the "Why me?" variety. I am learning to live with my questions instead of seeking immediate answers. Rainer Maria Rilke, in the book *Letters to a Young Poet*, reminds each of us

> to be patient toward all that is unsolved in your heart and to try to love the *questions themselves* like locked rooms and like books that are written in a very foreign tongue. Do not now seek the answers, which cannot be given you because you would not be able to live them. And the point is, to live everything. *Live* the questions now. Perhaps you

will then gradually, without knowing it, live along some distant day into the answer.[11]

Living the questions is an act of faith that answers will be provided when we are ready. This gift, as with all the gifts, is related to the gift of patience within a process. I recall a wise professor in seminary who continually encouraged us to ask the tough questions. He would remind us that, "Questions are answers in embryonic form." And so I am learning to live in the paradox of what is known and what is unknown. This enables me to be open to the mystery of how God may choose to work in my life.

PARADOX OF CHRONOS AND KAIROS TIME

Another paradox in which we all live as Christians is the tension between "chronos" time and "kairos" time. We order our lives by the clock, by chronos time. So many fail to realize the existence of another kind of time—a special time in which chronos time stands still, and the mystery of time transcends our daily living.

God acts and has acted in kairos time. Jesus' birth was a moment in time that changed all time. Emmanuel ("God with us") came to dwell with us, thus proclaiming that the kingdom of God is here, present with us. The more we can live in that in-between time of the present and the not yet, the more we are open to the mystery, to the gift of paradox. Our lives move between opposite poles; we become less judgmental as we learn to abide in the in-between space between chronos time and kairos time.

PARADOX AND POWER

I've also discovered paradox in the many uses and types of power. At times my healing depends upon my relinquishing control, becoming vulnerable and open to God's spirit. Power then becomes the capacity to suffer and to participate in the suffering of others. Power comes when we realize that we don't have all the answers, yet have faith that God is present in our vulnerability and pain. This relational power can result in surprising and creative outcomes.

But characteristic of paradox, at certain times the exact opposite is necessary and appropriate. At times we need to reclaim our rightful power, a power we have relinquished as we've conformed to others' expectations. I took assertiveness training while hospitalized. I have learned to recognize when it is important, for my own integrity, to assert my personal power in a positive way, trusting and acting on the power and guiding wisdom that comes from deep within my authentic self. I am learning to proclaim the truth that resides in the center of my being.

This proclamation requires risking rejection when I speak up about my convictions. It involves risking rejection if I confront someone. I continue to struggle in this area because I strongly desire peace, harmony, and the absence of conflict. This desire is usually stronger than my willingness to engage in a situation of potential conflict. The result is that I lose personal power and feel angry that I have let others decide what is best for me. I still live within the tension of using power in constructive ways.

PARADOX OF INDEPENDENCE AND DEPENDENCE

The paradox of independence and dependence also continues as a dominant theme. Because of my childhood experiences, I learned that I could cope by taking care of myself and not depending on others. I learned to value my self-sufficiency. Now I realize how much I lacked nurture as I was growing up. I have no memory of being held, rocked, or comforted by my mother as a child. So I learned to do without. Somewhere deep inside, I believe I thought that I did not deserve love and care.

However, depression forced me to depend on others for my personal safety and care. My experience of nurture and care while in the hospital and by my husband during my depression was a new and uneasy experience for me. When we feel unworthy of love and attention, it is difficult to allow ourselves to be dependent, to be a gracious receiver of the attention and care of others. Learning to receive is another "growing edge" of my journey.

Again, I have had to reclaim my independence as a strength. It has enabled me to be resilient and to continue on a difficult journey when many times I wanted to give up. But I also must learn to recognize the times when I need nurturing.

PARADOX OF DOING AND BEING

I have referred to the paradox between "doing" and "being" a number of times, which to me parallels the long-standing religious conflict between faith and good works. We often equate faith with "being" and good works with "doing." Both are essential to leading a Christian life. The paradox arises when we must discern which is most needful at the time. There is a natural flow of giving and receiving. We must receive God's grace in order to give freely to others. Sometimes we need to just be with God and not do anything; other times we need to make plans, work hard, and accept the responsibilities that come our way.

We need to have goals in life, but the paradox is that we also need to have a certain degree of detachment from those goals—to become more process-oriented than progress-oriented. We need a sense of security, but we also need to be free to face the unknown and the infinite future possibilities.

When we discover our authentic self, we become whole. The paradox is that we no longer center our life in the "I." Instead, community becomes essential, and we act out our compassion for others in our works. We move from "I" to "we," recognizing the interconnectedness of all life. A fundamental transformation from within transfuses our outward works with meaning.

The Gift of Creativity

OUT OF THE SHADOW came the surprising gift of creativity, particularly in writing poetry. Poems would suddenly emerge without effort and require minimal editing. I now understand that these poems were really prayers, prayers I felt compelled to put into words. They usually came when I was most vulnerable—often when I was struggling with some problem. Many poems were scribbled on scraps of paper, restaurant napkins, or whatever was available as I drove down the freeway not really thinking about anything. (I don't recommend this as a steady practice!) I soon learned to keep paper and pen close by to record any poems or ideas that suddenly popped into my head. This creativity differed from my past creative endeavors. It emerged from a center, springing forth with a spontaneity and freshness. My inner choice to bring new meaning and clarity to my life was the driving force behind this creativity.

We generally define creativity too narrowly. Julia Cameron's book *The Artist's Way: A Spiritual Path to Higher Creativity* has expanded my thought in this area. Cameron begins with the assumption that we all are naturally creative, but we have erected blocks—usually out of fear—that thwart the natural creative process. If we learn to move beyond our fear, the real artist will emerge. If we move beyond what we believe is expected or demanded of us to a place of trust in the new life that is striving for expression, the fear dissipates in the light of freedom. In our vulnerability, humility, and openness, God can use us. Our creativity then emerges from deep inside us without effort. Cameron's book includes a series of exercises to open those channels of creativity. She states, "What you are doing is creating pathways in your consciousness through which the creative forces can operate. Once you agree to clearing these pathways, your creativity emerges."[12]

Many of us live with a creative potential that we never realize. Some of us are "closet artists" who never share our draw-ings, our work with clay, our photography, our writings, or other creative forms of expression. Hildegard of Bingen made the observation that there is wisdom in all creative works. Getting in touch with our creativity is a way to understand our inner wisdom and to enrich our spiritual life.

Creativity is also essential to our healing. One of my favorite activities in the hospital was art therapy. I loved to go to that room and create whatever felt right that day. I recall receiving great satisfaction from mindlessly painting sun catchers. It allowed me to forget my problems and just "be" in the moment. Everyone received sun catchers that Christmas! I sensed a deep satisfaction in being able to produce something that I could give to a loved one. Even in the shambles of my life, creating empow-ered me.

The most important creative activity is the ability to envision our own lives in a new way. We erect so many barriers to dis-covering new possibilities for living. Our frustration mounts when new ways of "being" in the world don't seem to work. We become hostile or angry when things do not go our way. Openness to God's creative spirit moving through us and through the uni-verse helps us level the barriers to creativity in our lives.

CREATIVITY THROUGH SELF-DISCOVERY

Dr. Rosen, in his book *Transforming Depression*, cites case stud-ies in which he has used art therapy to enable depressed persons to confront their own darkness and the conflicting forces that sometimes cause turmoil within. In order to die to our false self, we must first discover those hidden forces that keep us from becoming the persons God created us to be. Dr. Rosen helps his patients expose those hidden forces through artistic expression. He likens it to a death process. Once we discover the forces that have gripped us, we begin the gradual process of letting go of the negative. As cocreators with God, we begin to build new ways of being. When we symbolically die to our false self, there is a time of mourning. Again we return to the grief process. But when the grief process has run its course, people experience new life and rebirth. With rebirth comes a renewed sense of purpose and meaning.

Dying and rebirth is a process we go through again and again. With each symbolic death, we either shed old values and attitudes, or we creatively transform those old values in ways that nourish and sustain our soul. Thus the process of rebirth becomes a movement from disintegration and fragmentation to one of integration and wholeness. When we allow ourselves to envision our lives in new and creative ways, we open ourselves to infinite possibilities.

CREATIVITY AND A QUICK-FIX SOCIETY

Our society does not encourage us to envision our lives in new and creative ways. Most people view depression as something to "get over," something to conquer or defeat as quickly as possible. Our society is so caught up in the quick cure. As insurance companies try to become more cost-effective, they cover less and less mental health care. Since my last hospitalization, my own HMO will only admit patients to a locked unit. I no longer have the option of a ten- to fifteen-day hospital stay with intensive therapy. The same phenomena has impacted outpatient therapy. The emphasis is on short-term therapy as a way of moving people through the system as quickly as possible.

Yet depression is not something to overcome or conquer or defeat. Making depression our adversary sets up a confrontational situation where there is a winner and a loser. In my experience, when I adopt a "battle mentality," I feel more disconnected from myself; and, consequently, more depressed.

Few persons regard depression as something to be "lived" that we might be transformed by God's grace. Yet the journey through depression offers an opportunity to learn and grow; and often, for the first time, to experience who God intends that we become.

In my own case, the gift of creativity, as well as the other gifts, would have remained buried had I not had the good fortune of a long-term relationship with my doctor and pastoral counselor.

CREATIVITY AND TRANSFORMATION

Understanding the gift of creativity as one path to transformation is spiritually much healthier than viewing depression as something we need to control or overcome. I am not an artist. So I had to stretch myself to take a workshop at a conference I attended, which forced me to engage in the creative process. I attended a workshop on creating mandalas. I sat for a long time and finally chose a black piece of paper. I lost track of time as I "created" a mandala that became an artistic outline for this book.

Only as I distanced myself from my creation was I able to see what my subconscious had produced. It was rich in symbolism: The black, of course, was the shadow. I had chosen the other colors for their special meanings: white for my authentic self; red for desire; green for growth; gold for the gifts awaiting discovery; brown for God's sheltering wings; and blue for water, both as a destructive and a healing force.

The shapes I chose also had symbolic meaning. The circular mandala symbolized the wholeness I desired. The spirals represented my desire to move through the shadow. The irregular splotches of green were opportunities for growth. The wave shapes signified the ocean with my suicidal ideations, as well as buoyancy that would allow me to float on the water. The flame shapes were fire. The feathery lines were God's wings. And the irregular golden shapes were the six gifts of the shadow that I describe in this book.

I returned to my room and wrote the outline for this book, which has remained virtually unchanged. The writing of this book was no longer a matter of choice but an imperative. I needed to honor that imperative for my own healing. I needed to speak my truth. I needed to provide an avenue for the creative potential I felt, or I might never have expressed it.

Art created by others can also connect us to and ground us in the larger community. Art bypasses our rational, intellectual side and speaks directly to our soul. Art can bring a sense of order to our chaotic inner world. When I can lose myself in a painting, a sculpture, or music that stirs my emotions in some inexplicable way, those creations become another source of healing.

I'm reminded of the creation stories in Genesis. God created the world and human beings out of chaos and darkness. God created, and it was good. The times I find myself groping in the darkness with no sense of who I am, I envision God in the mud, creating and molding a child. I envision allowing myself to trust the process and to cooperate with God in this new creation. And surprisingly, I discover that Susan is good!

The Gift of Hope

CHANGE IS PART OF LIFE. All of creation is in the process of change. One of the gifts of depression is that depression forces us to abide in our darkness; to face our doubts, regrets, and failures. In that process, we can become more aware and alert as to how God is changing and transforming us. Therefore, hope may exist in tension with the despair we feel in our lives. In the uncertainty of change, we can learn to reach beyond our personal pain and to place our trust in a process of salvation for all creation that is much greater than our individual struggles.

I can write this only when I am through the worst of my depression (at least for a time) and can, therefore, look back and realize what it has meant. I could not have written this book when things were really bleak; when my only desire was to run away, to retreat from the world, to get relief from the emotional pain.

But having been forced by depression to go inward and downward to the depths of my own being, I discovered that I was not alone. When we are so far down that we feel total emptiness inside, we mysteriously arrive at a still center point. There we experience a calm and peace in letting go, knowing that we are totally dependent on God for our salvation. In that resting place, God's sheltering wings cover us until we are ready to awaken to life again.

RUNNING WITH PERSEVERANCE

And when we transcend the depths of our personal pain, we can look back and realize that we have persevered. I am reminded of these words from Hebrews:

> Therefore, since we are surrounded by so great a cloud of witnesses, let us also lay aside every weight and the sin that clings so closely, and let us run with perseverance the race that is set before us, looking to Jesus the pioneer and perfector of our faith (12:1).

Paul certainly knew what it was to endure hostility, to struggle against those things that would defeat us, and to endure all sorts of trials. And, like Paul, we are part of that supportive cloud of witnesses whether we realize it or not.

To a person deep in despair these thoughts only make the person feel more like a failure. But when we have endured certain trials in our lives and can look back with a sense of perspective, we gain a sense of hope. Because we have made it this far, we will be able to persevere in the future. Again we are dealing with paradox. Sometimes we need to let go and be present to our pain. Letting go, however, is not giving up. Suicide would have been giving up. Letting go is also not apathy or passivity.

My childhood experiences taught me perseverance and determination. Yet in the midst of my depression, I lost my ability to persevere. I could barely hang in there in times of great pain. I began to view my childhood patterns of perseverance and determination as negative, something I needed to eliminate.

As healing took place, I was able to reclaim perseverance as a positive attribute. I felt hope that I could survive the hardships in my life. Hope then became a conscious decision to live each day in expectation and anticipation of what was to come.

REMEMBERING

Now when I begin to feel down, I remember. Remembering is one way to keep hope alive. In the article "How Long, O Lord?", Elizabeth Canham writes,

> Remembering makes the waiting time more bearable, for it fills the present emptiness with hope and allows God to be bigger than the present moment might suggest.[13]

In my times of darkness, I not only remember my own journey but also find hope in listening to and reading stories of healing and wholeness in other people's lives. Many of us have experienced a sense of empowerment that follows a deep darkness. Many of us can look back and realize how we have been reshaped and transformed while in the shadow. Most who have gone through such experiences agree that it takes great courage to die to old patterns and behaviors and to begin to confront new challenges with a renewed sense of hope. Jesus tells us that only as we become as little children can we view our future with a freshness and an expectancy of possibility, wonder, and hope.

EXPECTING THE GOOD

Like all gifts of the shadow, this gift of hope is not linear—something we can only expect in the future. Hope is not simply positive or wishful thinking that problems will turn out all right. Hope is not escapism. It is not tied to religious doctrines or dogmas but emerges from a place deep inside.

Hope is expecting that we will experience good in our present. Hope is grounded in the steadfastness of God who has acted in our past, is acting in our present, and will continue to act in our future. Therefore, hope becomes both a present and a future reality when we acknowledge our involvement with God in the process of personal transformation.

Realizing that God has been with us all along, involved in the process of our own recreation, is truly a God-given gift. I often glimpse moments when I recognize that little changes have occurred in my life. I feel that I am part of the mystery of all creation. I experience it as a homecoming. Like the prodigal son, we have been in a far country—exiled and suffering from a famine of the soul. Hope is knowing that we can come home and that God will welcome us with all God's riches.

Coming Home

O God, the journey has been so long.
I've taken every side road along the way.
I've explored all the hidden places.
As your prodigal daughter,
I've felt that I could find the way myself.

Even so, You, as loving parent, were beside me
> *picking me up when I fell*
> *sustaining me when my strength was gone*
> *nurturing me when I was helpless.*
And when I was exhausted
> *floundering*
> *ready to give up,*
You touched me with Your grace,
And I felt Your abundant love.

We walked back home together . . .
> *hand in hand.*

5 Emerging from the Shadow

E MERGING FROM THE SHADOW is a gradual process. And while not without its gifts, it is also laden with risks. The story of Bartimaeus bears witness to this fact. As I became healthier, the story that relates the healing of Bartimaeus intrigued me. (Read Mark 10:46-52.) Bartimaeus was a man who, like many of us, had been living in darkness, a literal darkness. Mine was a darkness of the spirit and the soul.

Who was Bartimaeus? All the text tells us is that he was a blind beggar sitting by the roadside. But from that simple information, we can surmise a number of things. Bartimaeus was probably alone, isolated from his community. In those days, persons perceived sickness of any kind as God's punishment. So in the crowd's view, he must have been some kind of sinner.

People were supposed to give alms. So Bartimaeus functioned as someone who allowed the people to fulfill their religious obligations. All the codependents could care for him!

But there is much more to this man Bartimaeus. He was willing to make himself vulnerable. He was willing to take risks. He clearly knew what he needed from Jesus. Perhaps Bartimaeus was fed up with his role as a roadside beggar; perhaps he was ready for a change in his life.

Bartimaeus's wounds allowed him to be vulnerable enough to approach Jesus and ask for mercy. When we are most desperate and are able to give up the illusion of control, we, like Bartimaeus, can accept the gift of vulnerability. Bartimaeus did not ask for healing first; he asked for mercy. It was a cry for relationship.

What happened? The crowd rebuked him, "Don't rock the boat. Get back where you belong." It embarrassed them that he was calling attention to himself in front of Jesus. Maybe the people in the crowd were a little jealous. Maybe they would have liked mercy too, but they worried that there might not be enough to go around. Perhaps they understood mercy to be a limited commodity rather than an abundant gift of God.

The crowd's rebuke did not stop Bartimaeus; he cried out all the more. He was serious, persistent, and probably quite desperate. This may be his only chance, and he had lived in darkness long enough. He was tired of being a victim.

What did Jesus do? He brought everything to a halt and created a space for Bartimaeus; Jesus stopped everything for one small voice. The crowds were pushing and surging along. When Jesus stopped, we can imagine everyone's tripping over one another. Jesus says, "Call him here." The crowd is stunned, bewildered, confused. The very people who only moments ago were telling Bartimaeus to be quiet, are now placed in the position of calling to the blind man, saying, "Take heart; get up, he is calling you."

Bartimaeus threw off his mantle, arose, and sprang toward Jesus. For me, his simple action of throwing off his mantle is the key to the story: He threw off his old identity, leaving his security behind in the dust by the roadside. He risked and made himself vulnerable; Bartimaeus took action.

And Jesus asked the man directly: "What do you want me to do for you?" Jesus created more space for the man. Bartimaeus answered, "My teacher, let me see again." Bartimaeus requested what he needed. He blurted it out. He didn't sit down and take time to analyze his situation. Bartimaeus participated in the healing process by being specific in recognizing and stating his need. He received his sight and followed Jesus.

RISK-TAKING IN THE DARKNESS

We all have mantles that we need to throw off and cast aside in order to open ourselves to Jesus' healing power. And if we can do that, can we take that second difficult step and ask for what we need? Let me tell you, it takes great courage to ask for what we need. It is easier to remain as we are. Bartimaeus demonstrated his faith in his action, in his persistence, in his taking the initiative, in his asking, and in his throwing off the mantle of all that bound and blinded him. Jesus told Bartimaeus that his faith had made him whole.

Sometimes getting what we ask for is more frightening than the asking. Again we find ourselves living in that paradox between security and risk-taking. Suddenly this man's life was changed. Others had related to Bartimaeus based on his blindness. Indeed, Bartimaeus's life centered around his blindness. How was he going to make a living? The pathology he depended on would work no more. He risked all with no guarantee that he would be healed. In times like these our wounds can be our strength. While outwardly blind, Bartimaeus had an inner strength and vision that comes only with faith.

As I emerged from the shadow, my life—like that of Bartimaeus—began to change. My changes were not as dramatic. As I changed, our family dynamics began to change—especially for those closest to me who had organized their lives around my depression. This was, and continues to be, a period of uncertainty. "Is Mom really OK?" "Can she handle this crisis without retreating into darkness?" "Is it safe to bring friends to the house?"

As my family and those persons close to me experienced my increasing health, I sensed a collective sigh of relief. Our relationships and activities were now moving back to normal. But inside there is still a fragility and a fear that I live with every day. Will something come my way with which I will be unable to cope? Will I sink back into the depths of depression?

I've done such a good job of covering up my pain in my depression that I have to remind my family that, despite my healing, I am still vulnerable. To some extent, I will always be vulnerable to criticism, rejection, and the feeling of abandonment. But I accept that limitation and am learning to live into those feelings when they come my way.

As an Easter people, we are often quick to throw off our mantles and move to new life and resurrection. We forget that new life is demanding and even threatening. Julia Esquivel has written a collection of poems entitled *Threatened with Resurrection*. Think about that for a moment. Threatened with resurrection! Esquivel is a native of Guatemala, where she was an elementary school teacher. Her commitment to justice put her on the wrong side of Guatemala's government, and she was forced into exile. In her poetry Esquivel shares her experiences of oppression as a Latin American, as a woman, and as an advocate for children.

Parker Palmer, in his book *The Active Life* speaks of Esquivel's writings and relates them to his own experience. Palmer refers to his struggle with depression and tells how depression gave him "a legitimate reason for hiding out from the world of action and decision and responsibility."[1] He goes on to say, "If we—people like me and perhaps you—really believed in resurrection, believed it not just in theory but in our bones, we would have no choice but to risk all that we have."[2]

Isn't that what Bartimaeus did? He risked all he had for a chance at new life. The only way to get to that new life, that resurrection, is to pass through a kind of death. The only way to accept the gift of healing is to face the threat that change inevitably brings.

Resurrection threatens many arenas in our lives. Our mantles are well-worn; casting them aside would make us uncomfortable. A person must be ready for healing. I needed many of the mantles I wore in depression, and it is a wise counselor who allows a person to wear those mantles until he or she is ready to let them go. No one can bring you to that point until you are ready. We don't know how long Bartimaeus sat by the roadside in his personal darkness. But Bartimaeus had come to the point in his own life when he was ready to ask for healing and new life, and that day he boldly asked Jesus, "My teacher, let me see again."

PRAYER IN THE DARKNESS

Many persons have asked me about the importance of prayer in the darkness. In the depths of my darkness, I could not formulate words of prayer, much less ask God for what I needed. I had no idea what I needed. As I began to emerge from the shadow, I could articulate my needs more easily. As a pastor, I have found that many people are reluctant to be specific in prayer and to ask for what they need. People often lament, "Well, God already knows what I want." Or, "What if what I want isn't what God wants?"

This reluctance to be specific surfaces especially in prayers for healing. Perhaps we fear that God will not answer our requests. But that does not preclude our offering specific petitions, if we can. Underlying all healing is the establishment of a relationship with God and a tapping into the great mystery of God's love for us. Our prayers for healing help us trust in God's promise to be with us in the midst of our suffering. We begin to recognize God's sustaining presence in pain, sickness, injury, and estrangement.

Prayer brings us into healing reunion with our Creator. Physical healing sometimes takes place. Mental and emotional balance are often restored. Spiritual health is enhanced through healed relationships. Prayers for healing change us and make us new. After Bartimaeus received his sight, he followed Jesus on the way. His life would never be the same. But his faith gave him the courage to face change, to face an uncertain future, and to receive the healing and wholeness God intends for each of us.

I recognized the importance of prayer and maintaining a relationship with God, even when sensing only God's absence. I began to formulate services of healing during which people could come forward, state their need, and be anointed with oil. The response to these services was overwhelming.

Persons' coming forward in these services and asking for what they needed deeply moved me. I felt the sacredness of each person's petition. In that environment, parishioners shared concerns they would never talk about in a formal counseling session. By placing the service of healing in a liturgical setting, it served as a confessional.

During one of those services, I realized the need to confess my own brokenness—not just to those few persons who already knew what I was going through—but to my church community. After another hospitalization, I decided to openly acknowledge my depression in order to facilitate my own healing. I wrote the following article for our church newsletter entitled "The Burden of Silence."

> I am speaking out on behalf of the millions of persons who suffer from some form of mental illness. I have struggled with clinical depression for over two years, my depression being precipitated by unresolved childhood issues. I recently spent eight days in the hospital and am currently attending a day treatment program twice a week. Those who have suffered with depression or who have had a family member with depression know the pain of this illness.
>
> I am speaking out to help erase the stigma of mental illness. Depression is an illness, like diabetes or cancer, that is caused by a chemical imbalance in the brain. The good news is that there are many effective treatments available. The bad news is that shame, guilt and fear prevent many persons from seeking the help they need.
>
> Many prominent persons who suffer with depression and receive proper treatment, continue to function in their jobs and in their personal relationships. Our new Parish

Nurse is a good resource if you think you are suffering from some form of mental illness—depression being the most common. To quote from "A Voice for the Voiceless—The Church and the Mentally Ill": "People with mental problems are our neighbors. They are members of our congregations, members of our families; they are everywhere in this country. If we ignore their cries for help, we will be continuing to participate in the anguish from which those cries for help come. A problem of this magnitude will not go away. Because it will not go away, and because of our spiritual commitments, we are compelled to take action."[3]

And so as I share with you my own struggle with depression, I ask that you would keep me and my family in your prayers as I seek the wholeness and healing in my life that God intends for us all.

So many people responded with their own stories that we held an informational meeting on depression with a turn-away crowd of over 130 people. Seeing such a great need, our parish nurse and Care Council facilitated a depression support group at our church. That group has expanded to include persons facing dark times other than depression. My painful experience has empowered others to receive the help and support they need.

SETTING HEALTHY BOUNDARIES

I also learned that I needed to set healthier boundaries. I knew I was still vulnerable and was not in a position of strength to make myself available to the many people in my congregation suffering with or dealing with depression. Two church members who are licensed social workers volunteer their services to work with these groups. I know that I am continuing to heal and that my emerging self is still vulnerable. In many ways, the protection I felt of being in the shadow had a great hold on me. Like Bartimaeus, it has not been easy to give up the security of the darkness.

In Crete the word for tomb means the "earth's womb." I was on a retreat at a Catholic retreat center, which had the stations of the cross. Arriving after dark, as I looked out my window, I could see a lighted cross in a grove of trees. Its beauty inspired my vow to explore the area first thing in the morning. And so the next morning I got up early to visit "my cross." Much to my surprise, I found that it was the final station of the cross and that hidden in the trees, down some stairs, was an actual tomb. I peeked into the small crawl space that led to the tomb. It was dark, dank, and dirty. I left immediately and went to breakfast.

But the image of that tomb stayed with me as I listened to the retreat speakers. I stayed away from the tomb that first day. But the next day during our free time, I felt drawn to that space. Self-consciously I slipped in through the small opening. It was very cold, but I knew I had to stay. Slowly I sat down in the corner, leaning against the stone walls. A soft stream of light came in through the small opening; and as my eyes adjusted, I could see that people had tied bits of ribbon and colored cloth to the supporting beams inside. There was also a seven-day devotional candle that had never been lit.

I wasn't sure what to do, or why I was even there. The sound of my breath seemed to fill the space and vibrate off the stone walls. There was life in the tomb—the breath of life—my life. I sat in the tomb for what seemed to be a long time. The first thing I saw upon emerging was the chapel cross. The warmth of the sun's rays quickly replaced the coldness of the tomb. I knew that I was entering another phase of my depression—that of emergence and healing.

The tomb became the focus of my retreat days. The following day I took some matches with me when I visited "my" tomb. After a period of time in the dark silence, I lit the candle, and the tomb glowed from its light. For the rest of the retreat, I became the "keeper of the flame." An internal pull urged me to keep the flame going. I would check the candle several times a day and at night before bed. The last thing I did as I left the retreat center was to check the candle. I left with the knowledge and hope that God's light is present even in our darkest times.

GOD'S PLANS

I believed that breaking the burden of silence about my own depression to my church congregation and the forming of the support group would be enough; I had done my part. I could now back off, continue with my therapy and healing, and put more energy into my church responsibilities. But God had other plans! During this time I received a phone call from an organizer of our annual bishops' convocation. This person, who also happens to be a dear friend, asked if I would present a workshop on "Understanding Depression" to my colleagues at that convocation. She said I had some time to pray about it, but the planning committee really needed to know as soon as possible.

I remember hanging up the phone, certain that I could never do such a thing. But an inner voice said that I had no choice. If I were to trust my emerging authentic self, I had to listen to what it was telling me to do. Before I could talk myself out of it, I called my friend and said "Yes." With that I was committed.

As I worked to prepare my talk, I had moments of regret. Those old demons of fear of rejection or abandonment by the church lurked in the background. After all, this was a bishops' convocation! And these were my colleagues in ministry!

I grew more nervous as the time approached for my workshop. As the room filled with people, I shut the door to ensure confidentiality for myself as well as for others. I don't remember much about the presentation. Once I began, I had a sense of being carried through it all. Suddenly the workshop was over, and colleagues I didn't even know were thanking me and sharing their personal stories of pain and silent suffering.

The pain of my colleagues that day grounded my commitment to working for healing within the religious community. I realized that I no longer had a choice. Personal healing is only the first step. As I became more whole and more integrated myself, I became more aware of how interwoven and interconnected we all are; all of creation is bound together. What began as an inward journey of self-discovery has gradually led me back to community and caring for others. I needed to live out the compassion I was feeling for others in the community. Parker Palmer states it this way:

> For many of us, the life we need to lose is life lived in the image of the autonomous self, and the life we shall then find is that of the self embedded in community—a community that connects us not only to other people but to the natural world as well.[4]

Palmer goes on to say,

> Paradoxically, as we enter more deeply into the true community of our lives, we are relieved of those fears that keep us from becoming the authentic selves we were born to be.[5]

Emerging from the shadow is elusive—it doesn't happen all at once. For me emergence continues to be a series of mini-epiphanies. Epiphanies—manifestations or revelations—are those moments when our senses are opened to the sacredness of the moment.

RECENTLY, DURING THE SEASON OF EPIPHANY, I had the opportunity to visit our daughter, Sarah, who was studying in England. I thoroughly enjoyed the trip and realized that I was not only present to what was going on, but I was also having a great time.

We took care to avoid tourist attractions and to see the "real" England. Consequently, we spent a lot of time getting lost in the Underground or waiting for the Badger buses! My only request was to see Stonehenge, a mysterious and ancient configuration of stones found in England. The sacred mystery surrounding that place has always been a draw. So I talked my daughter into a trip to Stonehenge—not an easy undertaking in the dead of winter with train tracks flooded out and unpredictable bus schedules.

To our delight, virtually no one was there. The area was free of "wannabee" Druids and street vendors. In the biting cold, we wrapped our scarves around our heads and ventured through the tunnel and up the path to Stonehenge. We stood there in awe and silence, taking in the sight of this strange configuration of stones. I don't know what drew me to this place, but since no one knows for sure what this strange circle of rough-hewn stones signifies, I sensed that I was in good company. Maybe I was learning to live those unanswered questions.

To appreciate this bleak place, one must have a yearning for mystery. One can only wonder why people would work together to roll these huge rocks to this expansive plain from as far away as 130 miles. How did they move those seven-ton stones and place them on top of other stones? Ancient peoples had expanded and "redecorated" Stonehenge three times before 150 B.C. The original stones came all the way from Wales.

Many theories have been proposed as to the purpose and meaning of this place. Evidently it was some sort of spiritual center where priests carried out their various duties. Some have speculated that the configuration of the rocks was somehow linked to the yearly cycle of the sun. As I stood there in silence, I felt a new sense of peace and integration, a sense of being tied to these ancient peoples in some mysterious way. Then it dawned on me. We, the children of the Enlightenment, have lived with disintegration, with the conflicting separation of faith and reason for 300 years. We have relegated religion and science to separate, isolated spheres. Western culture has viewed faith and reason as mutually exclusive rather than interrelated.

In my depression, I too viewed things as either/or. But standing on that freezing plain, I was whole! For these ancient peoples there was no separation between science and religion, between the sacred and the profane. The detachment that I felt so often in my depression gave way to a sense of integration. It was a personal epiphany!

Rituals

I have come to recognize our need to acknowledge our personal epiphanies and other milestones in our lives through ritual. We all have powerful moments related to births, weddings, funerals, graduations, and confirmations. But often these rites of passage or rituals are years apart. Our souls need daily nourishment; ritual, ceremony, and symbol bring us closer to ourselves, to one another, and to God. Rituals, especially when rooted in everyday experience, can be transforming.

Robert Fulghum, in his book *From Beginning to End: The Rituals of Our Lives*, talks about public, private, and secret rituals that bring structure and meaning to our lives:

> From beginning to end, the rituals of our lives shape each hour, day and year. Everyone leads a ritualized life: Rituals are repeated patterns of meaningful acts. If you are mindful of your actions, you will see the ritual patterns. If you see the patterns, you may understand them. If you understand them, you may enrich them. In this way, the habits of a lifetime become sacred.[6]

Ritual puts us back into life itself; it reconnects us. The holy becomes manifest in the sacred ordinary of daily life. Rituals enable us to make transitions in our lives. As I have emerged from my own shadow, I have used ritual and symbol to mark my journey.

Private Rituals

As I mentioned, our daughter studied in England for a year. Letting her go was difficult for me. When Sarah was a young child, we started a doll collection. Each Easter she would receive a new doll to add to our collection. And when the men in the family were not around, we would get out all the dolls and have a tea party. We would bake cookies especially for the occasion.

Each doll had her place on the dining room table with her own china tea cup and cookie. Of course, we had to consume all the cookies, leaving no evidence of our secret ritual!

Packing for my daughter's trip to England seemed like an endless process. There were arguments over what to take and what to leave behind. We sorted through her belongings. As we worked, I felt a deep sadness that my daughter no longer needed my advice—or me. Her excitement about her upcoming adventure encouraged me to keep the growing sadness to myself.

A few days before she was to leave, Sarah came to me and asked if we might have a tea party before she left. And so we did. There were more tears than tea, since our ritual allowed us to connect before our separation. We were sharing our love.

My daughter's departure was hectic. With one flight cancellation and the rush to find another in time to connect with her overseas flight, there was no time for lingering good-byes. I had no time to speak the words that were in my heart. But because of the tea party, I knew that Sarah knew what we both felt.

We got home late from the airport, and I went to bed. I awoke at 4:00 A.M., got up, and embarked on another ritual I cannot fully explain. I totally cleaned Sarah's room, which the day before had been strewn with boxes and suitcases. I stripped her bed and washed everything—dust ruffles and all. I took down her curtains and washed those. I vacuumed, dusted, and even washed the walls. I did not stop to eat or rest until I had completed this ritual cleaning. Hours later, I emerged from my daughter's room feeling refreshed and renewed. The transition was complete.

Public rituals

As Fulghum pointed out, it is not only our private or secret rituals that bring deep meaning to our lives but also public rituals. Church rituals are rich with symbolism and mystery. The sacramental ministry of the church is the most meaningful part of my role as minister.

And so it was only natural that while visiting my daughter in England, we sought out Evensong at Canterbury Cathedral. We went to Evensong at the cathedral both days I was there. The choir conveyed the awesome power in that enormous structure, which surrounded us with "a great cloud of witnesses."

As we continued our travels through England, we saw many beautiful cathedrals. We spent our last night in Oxford. It was cold and drizzly, typical English weather for that time of year. We managed to get lost! In our wandering, we happened onto a sign board on the street that announced a sung Eucharist Evensong at Christ Church Cathedral, the church where John and Charles Wesley were ordained priests in the Anglican Church. We decided to go.

As we walked into the church, I knew we had made the right decision. I felt strangely drawn to this place so rich in history. The church was not as grand as Canterbury Cathedral, and it was quite dark. But the candlesticks were lit in the choir loft, emanating a soft light that cast unusual shadows on the stone walls and pillars.

The students were still on holiday, and not many persons attended the service. But as the choir entered, voices filled the empty and dark spaces of that church—and of my soul. As the service progressed with the singing of the ancient but familiar creeds, I once again entered kairos time. Time stood still as I experienced a deep connection with all who had gone before, with my daughter kneeling beside me, and with myself.

All of the spiritual gifts of depression became available to me in that brief moment of time. As we made our communal and personal confessions, I entrusted my whole being into God's care. As the drama of the Eucharist liturgy progressed, the gift of my authentic self was affirmed. God loved and accepted me just as I was. I was able to relax into the familiar words as I received the gift of patient waiting, knowing that God was, is, and always will be working in my life.

As I knelt at the altar to receive the elements, I knew that I could live the unanswered questions offered by the gift of paradox and mystery. Listening to the haunting music, seeing the creativity expressed in the details of this church's architecture, stained-glass windows, altar adornments, I experienced a sense of deeply rooted community. And as we stood to receive the blessing and the benediction of the priest, I knew that I could persevere in the future with God by my side.

As my daughter and I walked out into the cold, dark night, I was grounded, connected, and filled with joy. David Adam's words from *The Eye of the Eagle* came to mind:

> We seem afraid of the shadows and the dark. We are unwilling to move out from our safe place. We do not like our securities or our ideas to be challenged. We are as afraid of a God that we cannot tame and control, as we are of being caught by the unpredictable in life.[7]

Adam goes on to say,

> It is when we go out from the safe and secure, when we reach over new boundaries, that we discover the God who is immanent and yet in the beyond. We are ever so afraid to let go, in case we lose control: we are afraid to stretch out in case we cannot return.[8]

Rituals and symbols often go together. When I made the difficult decision that I needed to write this book for my own healing and, hopefully, to help others, I looked for some time for a symbol to give meaning to that commitment. I did not know what I was looking for until I found it.

Again, a significant moment came while visiting with my daughter in England. There I saw a beautiful sculpture of a woman with her hands raised and her head thrown back in a gesture of pure joy. The artist had given the sculpture the title "Awakening." I knew that woman was myself. I was awakening to a sense of joy and enthusiasm with a renewed sense of purpose in my life. That awakening liberated me from bondage.

And so another ritual emerged—a ritual of relinquishment.

Ritual of Relinquishment

For four years I had held on to the "list" of messages from my mother's critical voice. I often wondered how and when I would be able to let it go. Acknowledging that I would never be entirely free from those messages, I knew instinctively that I needed to set them aside, to put them in a place where they would not hurt me as much. The list's strong hold on me required a special ritual. My pastoral counselor and I put much thought into its planning.

I selected the place: my private beach where I had fantasized about drowning in the ocean. I bought a pottery planter with a removable base. That pot sat in my garage collecting dust until a series of events let me know that it was time. My surrogate mother carefully selected a special, hardy plant. She chose one that changes colors in recognition of the changes occurring in my life.

The day of the ritual, I dug soil from my garden and packed the pot, plant, soil, and shovel into my car. As I left, I found a beautiful card my husband had placed in the plant, knowing the importance of this event in my journey. He wrote, "Today marks another milestone on your journey. I know how difficult this is for you. May you find some peace and closure in destroying the negative messages from your mother and may new life grow from the ashes."

At the appointed time I drove to my pastoral counselor's office. Together we moved all the items into his car and drove a short way to the ocean. February is usually a cold month, but God had pulled out all the stops: The day was warm and sunny. My pastoral counselor and I trudged down many steep steps, along a concrete retaining walkway, finally crossing some dirt to reach my own private rock. The seagulls expected food as they swooped around us. Instead, my counselor brought out "the list." He offered a prayer of relinquishment and blessing. I cried as I crumpled the list and laid it in the pot's base. We set it on fire. I kept crying as together we watched the list go up in flames and then turn to ashes.

I had brought some dirt from my garden at home. I also gathered soil from the surrounding beach. Together we mixed the soil with the ashes. After putting some of the dirt in the bottom of the pot, we lifted the plant into its new home and carefully placed the remaining dirt and ashes around the plant. I placed two rocks from Stonehenge on top of the soil.

As we sat back to contemplate what we had done, we needed no words. I sobbed quietly, grieving for my mother for the first time. I realize that one must love deeply in order to let go. Not only did I feel the release; but I suspect that she felt released as well. Jesus' words from the cross came to mind: "It is finished."

Driving home we both commented that it felt like we had attended a funeral. But we also felt uplifted because the time had come for my mother's release, and I needed to move on. The plant on my garden patio reminds me daily that new life does grow from the ashes.

MOST OF US WOULD NOT CHOOSE TO EMBARK on a journey into the dark night of the soul. But, in retrospect, I know that my depression forced me to become an explorer, a person who needed to discover who I was and to Whom I belonged. My emergence from the shadow is an ongoing journey of self-discovery, a journey that will take the rest of my life. The journey will involve some backward steps and setbacks, but I know deep inside that my healing continues.

Spirit God, you know our needs
                our wounds
                our hurts
                our fears
        even before we can form them
        into words of prayer.
You are patient with us.
You are protective of us.
You are present with us
        until such time that we are able
        to ask for what we need.
Thank you, Spirit God,
        for your healing taking place within
        before we are even aware
        of how broken we have become.

Notes

PROLOGUE

1. Frederick Buechner, *Telling Secrets* (San Francisco: Harper SanFrancisco, 1991), 30.

CHAPTER 1—INTO THE SHADOW

1. Walter Brueggemann, *Praying the Psalms* (Winona, MN: Saint Mary's Press, 1986), 17.

2. Robert A. Johnson, *Owning Your Own Shadow* (San Francisco: HarperSanFrancisco, 1993), 7.

3. Ibid., 17.

4. David Adam, *Tides and Seasons* (London: Triangle, 1989), 116.

CHAPTER 2—ABIDING IN THE SHADOW

1. William Styron, *Darkness Visible* (New York: Vintage Books, 1992), 84.

2. Harriet Goldhor Lerner, *The Dance of Anger* (New York: Harper & Row, 1986), 10.

3. Flora Slosson Wuellner, *Heart of Healing, Heart of Light* (Nashville: Upper Room Books, 1992), 73.

4. Ibid.

5. Dylan Thomas: *The Collected Poems of Dylan Thomas 1934–1952.* (New York: New Directions Publishing Corporation, 1971), 128.

6. Rosalynn Carter, "A Voice for the Voiceless—The Church and the Mentally Ill," in *Second Opinion* (Chicago: Park Ridge Center for the Study of Health, Faith and Ethics, 1990), 45–46.

7. Susan Gregg-Schroeder, "I Am Susan, and I Am Depressed," The Christian Minister (Chicago: Nov–Dec 1995), 28–30.

CHAPTER 3—GRACE IN THE SHADOW

1. Matthew Fox, *Original Blessing* (Santa Fe, NM: Bear & Company, 1983), 44.

CHAPTER 4—GIFTS OF THE SHADOW

1. Thomas Moore, *Care of the Soul* (New York: HarperCollins, 1994), 146.

2. Sandra Cronk, *Dark Night Journey* (Wallingford, PA: Pendle Hill Publications, 1991), Introduction.

3. Ibid., 10

4. Thomas Merton, *Thoughts in Solitude* (New York: Farrar, Straus & Giroux, 1984), 83.

5. Henri J. M. Nouwen, *The Wounded Healer* (New York: Image Books, 1990), 72.

6. *Diagnostic and Statistical Manual of Mental Disorders*, Fourth Edition (Washington, DC: American Psychiatric Association, 1994), 685.

7. Howard Clinebell, *Well Being* (SanFrancisco: HarperSanFrancisco, 1992), 3.

8. Macrina Wiederkehr, *A Tree Full of Angels* (San Francisco: Harper & Row, 1988), 26.

9. Sue Monk Kidd, *When the Heart Waits* (San Francisco: Harper & Row, 1990), 13.

10. Jean M. Blomquist, "To Touch the Fringe of God's Garment," *Weavings: A Journal of the Christian Spiritual Life,* 6, no. 4 (1991):35.

11. Rainer Maria Rilke, *Letters to a Young Poet* (New York: W. W. Norton & Company, 1993), 35.

12. Julia Cameron with Mark Bryan, *The Artist's Way: A Spiritual Path to Higher Creativity* (New York: G.P. Putnam's Sons, 1992), xiii.

13. Elizabeth J. Canham, "How Long, O Lord?," *Weavings: A Journal of the Christian Spiritual Life,* 6, no. 5 (1991): 24.

CHAPTER 5—EMERGING FROM THE SHADOW

1. Parker J. Palmer, *The Active Life* (San Francisco: Harper & Row, 1990), 141.

2. Ibid, 153.

3. Rosalynn Carter, "A Voice for the Voiceless—The Church and the Mentally Ill," in *Second Opinion* (Chicago: Park Ridge Center for the Study of Health, Faith and Ethics, 1990), 47.

4. Parker J. Palmer, *The Active Life*, 156.

5. Ibid.

6. Robert Fulghum, *From Beginning to End: The Rituals of Our Lives* (New York: Villard Books, 1995), opening page.

7. David Adam, *The Eye of the Eagle* (London: Triangle, 1995), 6.

8. Ibid.

Suggested Reading

Adam, David. *The Eye of the Eagle*. London: Triangle, 1995.

Adam, David. *Tides and Seasons*. London: Triangle, 1989.

Brother Lawrence. *The Practice of the Presence of God*. Uhrichsville, OH: Barbour & Company., 1993.

Brueggemann, Walter. *Praying the Psalms*. Winona, MN: Saint Mary's Press, 1986.

Buechner, Frederick. *The Sacred Journey* (1991); *Now and Then* (1991); *Telling Secrets* (1992); San Francisco: HarperSanFrancisco.

Burns, David D. *Feeling Good: The New Mood Therapy*. New York: William Morrow and Company, 1980.

Cameron, Julia. *The Artist's Way: A Spiritual Path to Higher Creativity*. New York: G. P. Putnam's Sons, 1992.

Cronk, Sandra. *Dark Night Journey*. Wallingford, PA: Pendle Hill Publications, 1991.

D/ART—Depression: Awareness, Recognition and Treatment Maryland: National Institute of Mental Health. (800) 421-4211.

Fulghum, Robert. *From Beginning to End: The Rituals of Our Lives*. New York: Villard Books, 1995.

Green, Thomas H. *Drinking from a Dry Well*. Notre Dame, IN: Ave Maria Press, 1991.

Green, Thomas H. *When the Well Runs Dry*. Notre Dame, IN: Ave Maria Press, 1979.

Jack, Dana Crowley. *Silencing the Self: Women and Depression.* Cambridge, MA: Harvard University Press, 1991.

Johnson, Robert A. *Owning Your Own Shadow: Understanding the Dark Side of the Psyche.* San Francisco: HarperSanFrancisco, 1991.

Kidd, Sue Monk. *When the Heart Waits.* San Francisco: Harper & Row, 1990.

Kübler-Ross, Elisabeth. *On Death and Dying.* Old Tappan, NJ: Macmillan Publishing Co., 1991.

Kushner, Harold S. *When Bad Things Happen to Good People.* New York: Avon Books, 1983.

Lerner, Harriet Goldhor. *The Dance of Anger.* New York: Harper & Row, 1985.

May, Gerald G. *Addiction and Grace: Love and Spirituality in the Healing of Addictions.* San Francisco: HarperSanFrancisco, 1991.

May, Gerald G. *Care of Mind-Care of Spirit: A Psychiatrist Explores Spiritual Direction.* San Francisco: HarperSanFrancisco, 1992.

Moore, Thomas. *Care of the Soul.* New York: HarperCollins, 1994.

Muller, Wayne. *Legacy of the Heart: The Spiritual Advantages of a Painful Childhood.* New York: Simon and Schuster, 1992.

Nouwen, Henri J. M. *The Way of the Heart: Desert Spirituality and Contemporary Ministry.* San Francisco: HarperSanFrancisco, 1991.

Nouwen, Henri J. M. *The Wounded Healer, Reaching Out, Creative Ministry.* New York: Continuum Publishing Co., 1996.

Palmer, Parker J. *The Active Life.* San Francisco: Harper & Row, 1990.

Rosen, David H. *Transforming Depression: A Jungian Approach Using the Creative Arts.* New York: Putnam Publishing Group, 1993.

Sanford, John A. *Healing Body and Soul: The Meaning of Illness in the New Testament and in Psychotherapy.* Louisville, KY: Westminster John Knox Press, 1992.

Sanford, John A. *The Kingdom Within.* San Francisco: HarperSanFrancisco, 1987.

Smalley, Gary and Trent, John. *The Gift of the Blessing.* Nashville, TN: Thomas Nelson, 1993.

Styron, William. *Darkness Visible.* New York: Vintage Books, 1992.

Thorne, Julia. *You Are Not Alone: Words of Experience and Hope for the Journey through Depression.* New York: HarperCollins, 1993.

Wuellner, Flora Slosson. *Heart of Healing, Heart of Light.* Nashville, TN: Upper Room Books, 1992.

Wuellner, Flora Slosson. *Prayer, Fear, and Our Powers.* Nashville, TN: Upper Room Books. 1989.

About the Author

SUSAN GREGG-SCHROEDER is coordinator of mental health ministries for the California-Pacific annual conference of The United Methodist Church. Prior to this appointment, she served thirteen years as minister of pastoral care and spiritual formation at a large urban church in San Diego, California. Currently Susan leads workshops, retreats, and conferences and develops resources in faith communitites to help erase the stigma and shame associated with mental illness. She is a certified pastoral care specialist with the American Association of Pastoral Counselors. She is married and has two grown children. Susan is the author of several books, including *For Your Hospital Visit: Prayers and Meditations for Children*, published by Upper Room Books.